Chris Flaherty

NIZAM-I CEDID: NEW ORDER ARMY INFANTRY & ARTILLERY, 1792 TILL 1807

SOLDIERS&WEAPONS 049

AUTHOR

Since 2009, Chris Flaherty has written for the UK Armourer Magazine; Classic Arms & Militaria; and, Soldiers of the Queen Journal. He has advised major international museums on uniforms. For Partizan Press in 2014, he wrote and illustrated two books: 'Turkish Uniforms of the Crimean War: A Handbook of Uniforms'; and, 'The Ottoman Army in the First World War: A Handbook of Uniforms'. He co-authored and illustrated with Bruno Mugnai for Soldiershop Publishing: 2014 'Der Lange Turkenkrieg (1593-1606), Volume. 1: The Long Turkish – War Habsburg Arrests the Ottoman Advance; and, in 2015 'Der Lange Turkenkrieg (1593- 1606), Volume. 2: The Long Turkish War'. In 2015, he was a contributor (illustrator) to the Turkish Gallipoli Centenary Exhibition: 'From Depths to the Trenches: Gallipoli 1915', at the Isbank Museum in Istanbul. He was one of the contributors to, 'Philip Jowett, 2015 Armies of the Greek-Turkish War 1919–22', Men-at-Arms 50, Osprey Publishing. He authored a chapter on the, 'Ottoman Army in the Great Northern War' appearing in Stephen, L. Kling, Jr. (Editor) 2016 GNW Compendium: A Collection of Articles on the Great Northern War, 1700-1721 (Volume: 2), The Historical Game Company. Chris Flaherty has authored and illustrated for Partizan Press' Universal Wargames Rules Supplements: 'Napoleonic Small Siege, River Ship, Gunboat and Pontooning' (2016); 'Napoleonic Foraging, Insurrection, Marauders, Bakeries, Convoy and Encampment Wargaming' (2016); 'Napoleonic Balloon Warfare' (2017); 'Napoleonic Ottoman Army Wargaming Supplement' (2018); 'A Wargamer's Guide to WW1 Ottoman Army Uniforms' (2018); 'Napoleon's July 1798 Pyramid Campaign & the Egyptian Army' (2019); 'The Napoleonic Ottoman Army: Uniforms, Tactics and Organization' (2019). Over 2021 and 2022 he wrote and illustrated several titles for Soldiershop Publishing, including: 'The Sardinian Expeditionary Corps'.

PUBLISHER'S NOTES

None of unpublished images or text of our book may be reproduced in any format without the expressed written permission of Soldiershop.com when not indicate as marked with license creative commons 3.0 or 4.0. Soldiershop Publishing has made every reasonable effort to locate, contact and acknowledge rights holders and to correctly apply terms and conditions to Content. In the event that any Content infringes your rights or the rights of any third parties, or Content is not properly identified or acknowledged we would like to hear from you so we may make any necessary alterations. In this event contact: info@soldiershop.com. Our trademark: Soldiershop Publishing ©, The names of our series & brand: Museum book, Bookmoon, Soldiers&Weapons, Battlefield, War in colour, Historical Biographies, Darwin's view, Fabula, Altrastoria, Italia Storica Ebook, Witness To History, Soldiers, Weapons & Uniforms, Storia etc. are herein © by Soldiershop.com.

LICENSES COMMONS

This book may utilize part of material marked with license creative commons 3.0 or 4.0 (CC BY 4.0), (CC BY-ND 4.0), (CC BY-SA 4.0) or (CC0 1.0). Or derived from publication 70 years old or more and recolored from us. We give appropriate attribution credit and indicate if change were made in the acknowledgements field.
All our books utilize only fonts licensed under the SIL Open Font License or other free use license.

ISBN: 9791255890133   1st edition September 2023
S&W-049 - NIZAM-I CEDID: NEW ORDER ARMY INFANTRY & ARTILLERY, 1792 TILL 1807
Written and illustrated by Chris Flaherty
Editor: Luca Cristini Editore, for the brand: Soldiershop. Cover & Art Design: Luca S. Cristini.

TIMELINE

1792	Omar Aga's Company formed, and grew into Levend Chiftlik Regiment.
	New Corps trained under instruction by Lieutenant-General Menant, Lieutenants Ranchoup and Luzin, along with six Sergeants sent by the French Ministry of War.
1793	Sultan Selim III ordered adoption of the Prussian drill system for Artillery.
	Infantry rifle muskets imported from France, England and Sweden.
1794	Boustangees (Sultan's Gardeners) Musketeer Regiment.
1796	Levy of twelve thousand men organized for the New Order Army.
	General Aubert du Bayet Military Mission arrived with Artillery equipment.
1798	Pamphlet published in Paris identifies the Pour le Corps discipline a l'Europeenne, de Levend Tchiftlik: European Discipline Corps from Levend Tchiftlik.
	French Mission in Constantinople sidelined due to French invasion of Egypt under Napoleon.
	British Artillery Sergeants in Constantinople instructing.
1799	Levend Chiftlik Regiment disembarked from HMS Tigre (8 May) landing at Gaza, at the 1799 Siege of Acre.
1800	British fleet blockade French in Alexandria, while 2,000 New Order Army Regulars, and 6,000 other Turkish troops land. Successfully blockading the French at Rosetta, forcing their surrender in April 1801.
1801-1802	Uskudar Regiment appears.
1804	New Order Army Regulars (under Kadi Abdurrahman Pasha) campaign against Mountain Bandit Forces in the Balkan and Rhodope Mountains. Established a Regulars' base at the town of Corlu.
	New Order Army Marines established, and organized into two 500 Soldier Regiments.
1805	Field Army Artillery standardized according to five different cannon calibre types.
1806	Edirne Rebellion sparked by resistance to New Order Army recruitment in the city of Edirne, in northwestern Turkey. First Incident of fighting between New Order Army Regulars and Janissary.
1807	Yamak: Bosporus fortresses Guards, deposed and imprisoned Sultan Selim III. The coup resulted in disbandment of the New Order Army.
1808	Brief restoration of Sultan Selim III and assassination, and enthronement of Sultan Mahmud II.

▲ Sultan Selim III in Audience, 1803[1].

---

1 Kapidagli, 1803.

INTRODUCTION

This book looks at uniforms, rank-system, and organization for a new type of Turkish Soldier, other than Janissary providing the main Soldier-type during the French Revolution, and Early Napoleonic Wars. Debut of the Levend Chiftlik Regiment in 1799, during the French siege of Acre, and in the British-Turkish campaign in Egypt to expel the French occupation, introduced the Nizam-i Cedid [Nizam-i Cedit; Nizam-i Jedid]: New Order Army. Having its beginning as part of the reforms of Sultan Selim III (1789 till 1807), several Anatolian Infantry Regiments, a Field Artillery Regiment, and two Galeonjees: New Order Army Marine Regiments came into existence. Arnaut: Albanian Infantry are looked at, as their military ethos, training, and organization appears to have had a strong connection with typical European Armies' style of warfighting. The book also covers late-18th Century Turkish Generalship and Officers' command; Standing Army's tactics; New Order Army Infantry Soldier's weapons and equipment; and, 1806 till 1807 events leading to the New Order Army's suppression and demise of Sultan Selim III.

1792 OMAR AGA'S COMPANY

Prior to the decision to create the New Order Army, around 1792, Sultan Selim III had tried to create two separate Corps: A Summer Warfare Corps drawn from Anatolian Cavalry, and Winter Corp: Standing Reserve consisting of Balkan Janissary[2]. The New Order Army generally has its origins in Omar Aga's Company, around 1792. An 1878 history states:

> "Among the prisoners made by the Turks during the last war, there was one who was a Turk by birth, but had long been in the Russian service, in which he had attained the rank of Lieutenant, and the reputation of a good Officer. The Grand Vizier Yusuf Pasha (by whose troops he had been taken), was fond of conversing with him on the military systems of the two nations; and was at last persuaded to allow a little corps (consisting chiefly of renegades) to be armed and drilled on the European plan."[3]

Omar Aga, the Russian Officer of Turkish birth, "[had been] … carried early in his youth to Moscow, he had become a Christian, and found in a Russian nobleman a patron who gave him a good education, and placed him in the Army."[4]

OMAR AGA'S CORPS (LEVEND CHIFTLIK REGIMENT)

The Capitan Pasha, Hussein, who, like the Sultan, saw the value of the new system, took some of them into his own service, and by high pay and patronage induced more local recruits to join Omar Aga's Company, expanding to a Corps:

> "These new troops were about 600 in number, when war broke out between France and Turkey, in 1798, in consequence of the attack which the French Republic, or rather Napoleon Bonaparte made on Egypt."[5]

In 1799, the Levend Chiftlik Regiment made its debut landing at Gaza, for the Siege of Acre. According to an 1878 history, "Omar Aga's little corps … acquired so much credit in the defence of Acre"[6].

---

2   Nicolle, 1998.
3   Creasy, 1878.
4   Eton, 1798.
5   Creasy, 1878.
6   Creasy, 1878.

THE 1792 AND 1796 FRENCH MISSIONS

The New Order Army, under Sultan Selim III, it is said, begins with the 1796 arrival of French Ambassador General Aubert-Dubajet [du Bayet]. The 1796 French Mission arrived with mostly Infantry Officers (depicted in a painting of the event[7]), who raised a Training Battalion. French Officers commanded the new French Training Battalion[8]. Future Turkish Army Officers and Non-Commissioned Officers developed. However, there was an earlier French Mission to train Infantry, by Lieutenant-General Menant, and his instructors in 1792[9]. What is not entirely clear, is how, and when Omar Aga's Company merged into the new French Training Battalion.

1799 EXPANSION

An 1878 history states that prior to 1799 two New Order Army Regiments, "uniformly armed and accoutered after the most approved French models, were now seen performing the same evolutions as those of the best European troops."[10] It is generally accepted that the first New Order Army Regiment was established in Levend in 1795, and the second one in Uskudar in 1799[11]; however, later dates of 1801, or 1802 are also given. The same 1878 history links the next phase of expansion with several Anatolian Regiments, created through the zeal of persons, such as Kadi Abdurrahman Pasha, Governor of Karaman [Carmania; Caramania], and commander of the Turkish Army during the 1806 Edirne Incident[12][13].

▲ A 1783 satirical cartoon shows French Instructors and Turkish Soldiers attempting Infantry drill[14]. It is more likely this scene relates to the 1792 French Mission under Lieutenant-General Menant.

7   Castellan, 1797.
8   Roubicek, 1978.
9   Shaw, 1965.
10   Creasy, 1878.
11   Uyar, 2009.
12   Shaw, 1977.
13   Creasy, 1878.
14   Anonymous, 1783.

1806 NEW ORDER ARMY'S ORDER OF BATTLE

By 1806 the following Infantry and Artillery could be identified forming the New Order Army:

INFANTRY
Omar Aga's Corps (Levend Chiftlik Regiment)
Levend Chiftlik Regiment (Levend Chiftlik Barrack's Training Regiment)
Boustangees (Sultan's Gardeners) Musketeer Regiment
Uskudar Regiment
Sultan's Household Infantry (Orta: Battalion)
ANATOLIAN SEGBAN PROVINCIAL MILITIA REGIMENTS
Aksehir Segban Provincial Militia Regiment (Uskudar Barracks)
Ankara Segban Provincial Militia Regiment (Uskudar Barracks)
Aydin Segban Provincial Militia Regiment (Uskudar Barracks)
Beygehir Segban Provincial Militia Regiment (Uskudar Barracks)
Bolu and Viransehir Segban Provincial Militia Regiment (Uskudar Barracks)
Kastamonu Segban Provincial Militia Regiment (Uskudar Barracks)
Kayseri Segban Provincial Militia Regiment (Uskudar Barracks)
Kutahya Segban Provincial Militia Regiment (Uskudar Barracks)
Nigde Segban Provincial Militia Regiment (Uskudar Barracks)
TOPCHEES: ARTILLERY
New Order Army's Topchees: Artillery Regimental Cannon Buluks: Company
Cannon and Howitzer Regiment-Brigade

HUMBARACI: BOMBARDIERS	
1st Humbaraci Regiment	4th Humbaraci Regiment
2nd Humbaraci Regiment	5th Humbaraci Regiment
3rd Humbaraci Regiment	

CHAPTER 1: NEW ORDER ARMY UNIFORMS

A major anomaly encountered in the study of early Turkish uniforms, is the relationship between the 1826 destruction of Janissary paraphernalia under Sultan Mahmud II, and a later 1850s work by a French artist who illustrated a collection of Janissary costumes found in the Elbicei Atika: Seraglio [Harem: The Women's Apartments in the Sultan's Palace] Armoury Museum of Costumes, in Constantinople[15]. It appears a set of costumes had been preserved, likely for use in theatrical productions for the Court's entertainment. It also appears, that by the time of Sultan Abdulaziz in the 1860s, that: "old Infantry dress … [could be] … seen in the Museum of Ancient Costumes at Constantinople"[16]. The first destruction, then rediscovery led to a historical jumble of uniforms, largely put out-of-order.

1850 ILLUSTRATIONS OF NEW ORDER ARMY REGULARS

Two sets of 1850 illustrations are known purporting to identify the New Order Army Regular's costume at the time of Sultan Selim III. The first 1850 group of figures, show the uniforms for: Artilleur-a-Cheval: Horse Artillery Soldier; Yuzbachi [Yuzbasi], Capitaine d'Infanterie: Infantry Captain, or Buluks: Company Commander; and, Artilleur-a-Pied: Foot Gunner[17]. However, potentially these figures could range in date from around the 1750s, till early 1826.

The second 1850 group of figures is said to cover the Ottoman Empire's military, and purport to show the uniforms for: Eghri Calpaklissi: Soldiers of the Reformation; Choubara Neferi, Soldat of the 1st Reform - Nizami Djedid Neferi: Reform of Sultan Selim; and, Choubara Neferi, Soldat of the 1st Reform of Sultan Mahmud II[18]. The uniforms depicted, show one figure wearing a tall tubular hat with a broad fur-plush band, a collarless white buttoned shirt, with a sleeveless yellow bolero jacket, with a heavy decorative silver trim, a red waist sash, yellow Russian pants, and red Turkish slipper-shoes complete the dress. The second figure, wear a small red quilted skull cap, with a red collarless jersey-jacket, with grey Russian pants, and low red Turkish riding boots completing the dress. The third figure also wears a red collarless jersey-jacket, with grey Russian pants, and red Turkish slipper-shoes, with a Boustangees' hat completing the dress. It is suspected, all the figures date to the later years of Sultan Selim III, to a few years after his death in 1808, till around 1810, and continued to be worn during the early-years under Sultan Mahmud II.

Another third group of uniforms illustrations depicting the Artillery, possibly covers an even wider date-range, often attributed to the Sultan Selim III Era, depicting: "Troupes Regulieres Turques – Artillerie"[19]. One of the figures: Artilleur-a-Cheval: Horse Artillery Soldier, may date to 1826, or may in fact be an older uniform for the 1790s, or be one that never changed over the intervening 30 years. The reason for this thinking, is that whereas three figures, in comparison to other illustrations, can be firmly dated to 1826 or 1828, the Artilleur-a-Cheval figure has a few anachronistic features, that seem out-of-place by 1826, such as display of French lace cravat more in keeping with the French Mission in Constantinople, around the 1790s where such a uniform item might have become popular – as the next new thing!

1798 UNIFORM

The 1798 Pamphlet recounts, "the State provides Officers and Soldiers with their arms and

---

15	Brindesi, 1850.
16	Slade, 1867.
17	Brindesi, 1850.
18	Brindesi, 1850.
19	Unknown, 1830.

uniforms"[20]. New Order Army uniforms are said to have been based on, "Austrian uniforms of the late 1700s"[21]. The similarity only goes so far, as unlike most European Soldiers dressed in the long or short tailed coatee with lapels, the Austrian Army introduced a simple single-breasted uniform jacket for its Infantry after 1767, which had a very short skirt, with front flaps folded-back, and a low soft collar. One other similarity with Austrian uniforms, was use of the peakless Kaskett, also adopted around 1767, that progressively became more a top hat, having close appearance to Turkish headgear over the 18th Century. Each New Order Army Infantry Regiments created had a distinctive uniform:

REGIMENTS	JERSEY-JACKET	HEADGEAR
Boustangees (Sultan's Gardeners) Musketeer Regiment (1794)	Pink	Boustangees' hat
Levend Chiftlik Regiment (1799)	Red	Red Cahouk, with a turban
Uskudar Regiment (1802)	Blue (with double sleeves)	Red bonnet with top tuft and turban
Sultan's Household Infantry	Yellow	Yellow Cahouk

An illustration of a New Order Army Soldier, dated after 1826, more likely earlier, due to the headgear, to be from around 1792 till 1807, with a caption identifying, "[a] … Soldier of the … [Boustangees] … or Corps from the Sultan's Gardeners"[22]. This depicts a figure wearing a pink collarless jersey-jacket with a double row of fine black lines edging, with grey Russian pants, and red Turkish slipper-shoes. A Boustangees' hat completes the dress. The 1798 New Order Army's Drill Regulations depict the same figure[23]. The use of a pink jersey-jacket rather than a red one (used by the Levend Chiftlik Regiment), points to a separation of the two Regiments around 1794, at the Levend Chiftlik Barracks.

Officers in the Boustangees (Sultan's Gardeners) Musketeer Regiment appear in 1798 New Order Army's Drill Regulations[24], and are depicted wearing long open coats, with long sleeves, that display: One pair of large chest buttons; Two pairs of large chest buttons, and carrying a small square flag on a short pole; Three pairs of large chest buttons; and, Four pairs of large chest buttons. All the Officers wear under the long coat a collared jersey-jacket with five tape chest bars, which appear to have buttons, a waist sash, Russian pants, and Turkish riding boots. A Boustangees' hat completes the dress. It is assumed, the chest bars end in tassels, as this feature is depicted in the 1907 illustration, described as, "Regne du Sultan Abdul … [Mahmud II] … Avan l'Introduction de l'Uniforme Europeenn": before the introduction of the European uniform[25].

An illustration identified as a Bimbachi: Chef de Bataillon du la Ref du Sultan Selim: Major - Chief of the Battalion, under Sultan Selim III[26], shows a long red collared coat, with long open sleeves, and four heavily embroidered chest bars ending in tassels. Red Turkish riding boots, and a Boustangees' hat completes the dress. Another similar figure appears in an illustration of the 1810 Sultan Mahmud II Grand Review[27], has yellow Turkish riding boots, and wears a purple waist sash, with seven embroidered chest bars ending in tassels visible. Colored waist sashes indicated a Boustangees rank status. Lowest grade wore rough cloth waist sashes[28]. Black silk waist sashes represented the eighth and ninth grades. By 1810, it appears to have changed to purple.

---

20 Raif, 1798.
21 Johnson, 1988.
22 Unknown, 1830.
23 Raif, 1798.
24 Raif, 1798.
25 Sevket, 1907.
26 Unknown, 1830.
27 Unknown, 1810.
28 Nicolle, 1995.

1st Grade	Blue	6th Grade	White Silk
2nd Grade	White	7th Grade	Fine Black Cloth
3rd Grade	Yellow	8th, and 9th Grades	Black Silk
4th Grade	Mixed Blue and White	9th Grade (1810)	Purple
5th Grade	Fine White Cloth		

Illustrations of the 1798 New Order Army Colonel show them wearing a long coat closed at the front by nine chest cords buttoned in the center, and have tasseled ends.

Levend Chiftlik Regiment Soldiers dressed in the French manner, with blue berets, red breeches and red jackets[29]. An 1850 illustration, showing a Choubara Neferi Soldat de la Reforme: New Order Army Infantry Soldier[30], shows a small red quilted cap worn[31]. In their Barracks New Order Army Soldiers wore the Boustangees' hat, but when on service they wore a lighter one[32]. A 1798 set of illustrations show the Soldiers wearing low collared jersey-jackets, Russian pants, Turkish slipper-shoes and Boustangees' hats. An 1803 illustration of a, "Turkish Foot Soldier", from the Egyptian campaign[33], possibly Arnaut: Albanian Infantry (sighted in Egypt in 1799), illustrates a figure wearing a Cahouk: quilted top hat, with a turban; and a short open red jacket, with yellow tape edging to the cuff-edge, and up the sleeve's back-seam, as well as wide blue breeches.

The uniform of the Uskudar Regiment: "the new ... [Uskudar] ... Regiment was given the color light blue for its jackets and breeches, to distinguish its Soldiers and Officers from those of Levend Chiftlik."[34] An illustration of a, "Soldier of the Ottoman Experimental Infantry, around 1802"[35][36]; also known as: "Nefer, Soldat des Nizam Djedyd": Soldier of the New Order Army[37]. This shows a blue collarless bolero jacket, with double sleeves, the other sleeves hanging from the back of the shoulders. Blue Russian pants, secured with plain blue leggings with a row of buttons connecting the backs. The figure also wears a red waist sash, red bonnet, with a top tuft, combined with a colored fringed shawl wrapped around it. Red Turkish slipper shoes complete the dress.

Jersey-Jacket

▼ The 1798 Pamphlet shows the uniform developed for New Order Army Soldiers[38], as a low soft collared (earlier versions appeared collarless), and buttonless loose-fitting jersey-jacket. Closed to the collar at the front by hidden buttons, or hooks and eyes. Stopped just below the belt, and had narrow sleeves, with low round cuffs. One version had rear hanging second sleeves. The back of the collar was cut into a downwards point triangle.

29	Shaw, 1965.
30	Brindesi, 1850.
31	Brindesi, 1850.
32	McLean, 1818.
33	Walsh, 1803.
34	Shaw, 1965.
35	Dalvimart, 1802.
36	Roubicek, 1978.
37	Castellan, 1812.
38	Raif, 1798.

Headgear

New Order Army Soldiers and Officers' wore the Boustangees' hat. The Boustangees' hat was a long red wool cloth tube, with a flat top. It may have had internal cardboard frames, which collapsed over time, due to wear. The New Order Army Regulars wore the Boustangees' hat:

> "[belonging] … nominally to the … [Boustangees] … at home, they wear the large red cap, which distinguishes that body; but on service, they wear a lighter one, as being better suited to field duty."[39][40]

The lighter version of the Boustangees' hat appears to have been a small red quilted skull cap. This is depicted in an 1850 illustration of a figure, said to be a Choubara Neferi, Soldat of the 1st Reform - Nizami Djedid Neferi: Reform of Sultan Selim[41]. It is also known, that:

> "In later times … [the Janissary Bork: hat] … was only worn by the men on occasions of parade or duty in their Garrisons; off duty and in the field, they wore a twisted white linen turban like that of the French Zouaves."[42]

The Cahouk: quilted top hat was worn. It had a wide-top with deep vertical lines of stitching forming pads. Commonly associated with the Sipahi: Cavalry, Mameluke, or higher-level Janissary Officers. An 1803 painting of Sultan Selim III in audience shows him wearing such a hat, with a white turban added[43]. Behind a raised top-brim the inner hat was dome-topped[44]. The Officer's version appears to have a low turban around the brow. The Cahouk, like the Caouk: turban[45], was made as a complete piece of formed or shaped headgear, which afforded its wearer a certain level of protection from edged weapons. It is also known, the Mameluke versions in Egypt incorporated a circle of metal as added protection[46]. According, to an account from Egypt in 1800, turban were so effectively constructed, that it apparently took great skill to even cut it with a scimitar, famed as these were for their immensely sharp blades, as it was: "composed of a mixture of wool and cotton, covered over with thick cloth, it required no little adroitness and dexterity to penetrate into its substance by a blow of the … [scimitar]."[47]

The last item of headwear worn was the "European hat" [48]. It has been noted, "[by] … the end of 1796 … members of the … [Levend Chiftlik Regiment] … were dressed in the French manner, with blue berets, red breeches and red jackets."[49] The only possible illustration of Turkish Soldiers wearing a French blue beret is a cartoon satirizing the 1783 French Military Mission[50][51][52]. The pre-1789 French Military Mission focused on Artillery development, naval warfare, fortification building training and engineering. Whereas Infantry training was more related to either the 1792, or 1796 French Missions. The 1783 (if that is the correct date, and it is not later – such as the 1792 French Mission under Lieutenant-General Menant) cartoon shows French Instructors wearing their bicorne hats, and Turkish Soldiers mostly wearing turbans, except with a training line, using wooden guns, wearing a type of tent hat, that has a striking resemblance to French Revolution Era Soldier's Fatigue Bonnets. A surviving example from 1790, shows this was a triangular fabric hat that ended in a tassel[53], with most of it folded-over on one side of the wearer's head.

39	Raif, 1798.
40	McLean, 1818.
41	Brindesi, 1850.
42	Tyrrell, 1910.
43	Kapidagli, 1803.
44	Brindesi, 1850.
45	Wittman, 1803.
46	Grant, 2007.
47	Wittman, 1803.
48	Sakul, 2012.
49	Shaw, 1965.
50	Anonymous, 1783.
51	Stolpe, 1985.
52	Aksan, 2007.
53	Metropolitan, 1790.

Pants and Footwear

New Order Army Soldiers and Officers universally wore Cossack trousers, otherwise known as Russian pants: a wide blooming pair of trouser. An 1829 traveller's account, stated the Cossack trousers: "are very wide down to the knee, where they are tied-in, thence they fit close to the leg, and descend to the instep."[54] It is also the case, that Albanian leggings were sometimes worn over the leg calves.

A similar pair of leggings are depicted in an 1812 illustration of a, "Nefer, Soldat des Nizam Djedyd": Soldier of the New Order Army[55]. This shows plain blue leggings with a row of buttons connecting the backs. One other variation appearing in illustrations are Russian pants with the lower leg buttoned tight. This was done by adding a line of closure buttons, either on the inside, or outside running-down the lower part of the pants legs.

New Order Army Officers and Soldiers wore two main types of footwear, either Turkish riding boots, or slipper-shoes commonly in red, yellow (in the case of high-status individuals), or black. Officers and Soldiers could wear their shoes, or boots barefoot or with white stockings.

WINTER CLOTHING

In general, the contemporary view was that the Janissary, "are by no means partial to winter campaigns"[56]. In Egypt, in 1800, it was noted by an English observer, how Janissary, "are occasionally enveloped by a loose cloak."[57] Protective clothing included the Aba: coarse wool cloak, and Kebe-i Yanbolu: coarse felt jacket[58]. A 1907 illustration of the Aba: coarse wool cloak, used by Janissary, is depicted gathered around the neck, and secured by a large button[59]. The cloak was possibly a large square wool blanket arranged to make a hood, cover the shoulders, and fall behind the back, allowing the wearer to pull the sides over the arms for greater warmth. Another 1907 illustration, in relation to 18th Century Turkish Sailors, give an indication of the Kebe-i Yanbolu: coarse felt jacket's appearance [60][61]. Depicted as a long yellow loose over coat with a hood, and heavy tape edging around the cuff-ends, down the front, and around the hood opening. Large red tape loops decorated the front.

1808 TILL 1809 NEW SEGBAN ARMY UNIFORMS

The New Segban Army (1808 till 1809) according to recent discussions, were dressed as New Order Army Soldiers[62]. It is possible that the post-1810 figures depicted in a set of 1907 illustration, described as, "Regne du Sultan Abdul … [Mahmud II] … Avan l'Introduction de l'Uniforme Europeenn": before the introduction of the European uniform[63], are some of these New Segban Army Soldiers, where the jersey-jacket was changed to yellow, and wearing yellow Cahouk: quilted top hats, while later-era uniforms, for 'European Model Soldiers' from around 1818, show Soldiers wearing red jersey-jackets with Boustangees' hats[64].

54	MacFarlane, 1829.
55	Unknown, 1812.
56	Valentini, 1828.
57	Wittman, 1803.
58	Sakul, 2012.
59	Sevket, 1907.
60	Sevket, 1907.
61	Basimevi, 1997.
62	Mugnai, 2022.
63	Sevket, 1907.
64	McLean, 1818.

NEW ORDER ARMY TRUMPETERS AND DRUMMERS

The Military Band was composed of several Music Officers, who played instruments themselves[65]. There was a Mehter Bashi: Music Master; Surnazen: Oboe player; Ser-Tabtzen: Drum Master, with a Mulazim-Ser-Nakarazen: small Tonbale player. Each Buluks: Company had a Sornazen: Trumpeter, and Tablzen: Drummer[66]. No special uniform distinction appears to be used, except carrying a drum or trumpet to indicate their rank. The drum type was likely based on French or British models with all brass construction. Later illustrations, after 1826, show Turkish Infantry drum sides painted blue, with plain brass hoops and white cords. The trumpet type used was likely a Turkish Boru: a brass trumpet-like instrument with an additional oval handle fitted, so the players' hand did not interfere with the instrument correctly vibrating (which could occur if they were directly holding it).

FIGURE 1: Soldier from the Training Battalion Period (1792).
FIGURE 2: Grenade badge details (1792).
FIGURE 3: Levend Chiftlik Regiment Sornazen: Trumpeter Soldier, holding a Turkish Boru decorated with small flags, and wearing a small red quilted cap (1796).
FIGURE 4: Levend Chiftlik Regiment Tablzen: Drummer Soldier, using a French Infantry drum, and wearing a French blue beret – the European hat (1796).
FIGURE 5: French Officer, Training Mission in Constantinople (1796).

---

65 Raif, 1798.
66 Shaw, 1965.

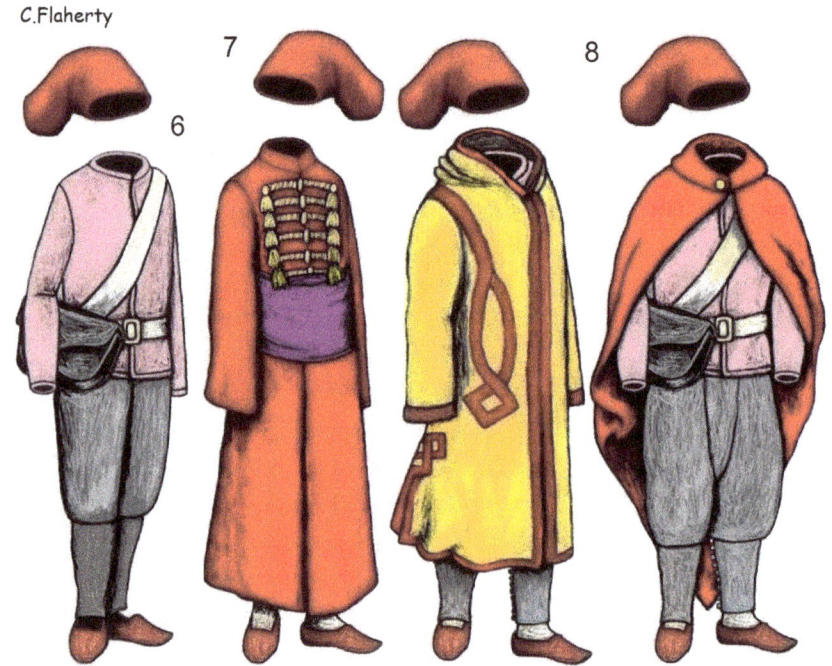

FIGURE 6: Boustangees (Sultan's Gardeners) Musketeer Regiment Soldier (1798).
FIGURE 7: Bimbachi: Chef de Bataillon, Boustangees (Sultan's Gardeners) Musketeer Regiment (1810).
FIGURE 8: New Order Army Regulars wearing Aba: coarse wool cloak, and Kebe-i Yanbolu: coarse felt jacket.

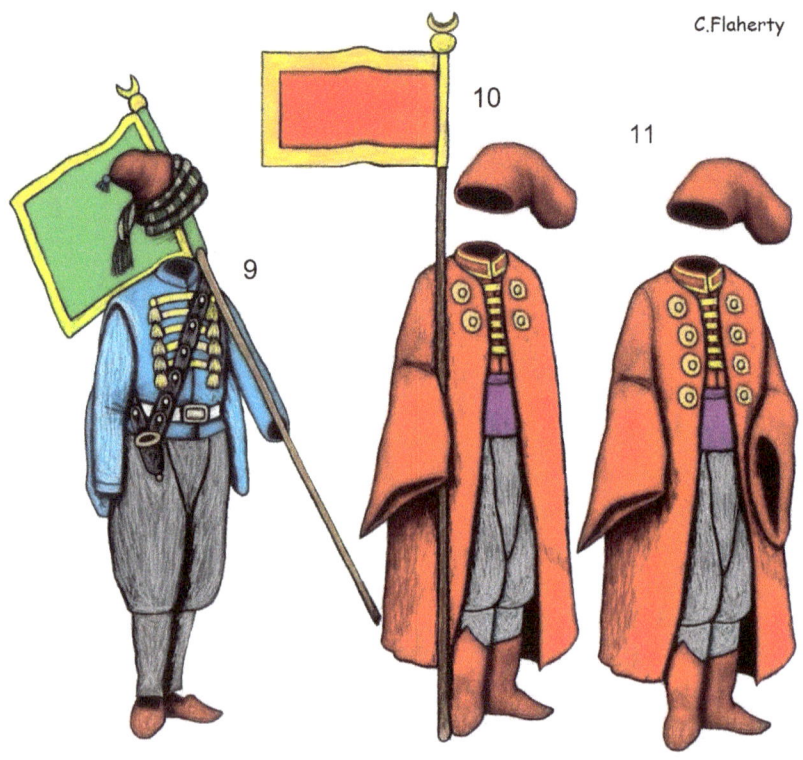

FIGURE 9: Reconstruction of a Uskudar Regiment Alemdar: Flag Bearer (1802).
FIGURE 10: New Order Army Regulars Alemdar: Flag Bearer, flag and pole details (1798).
FIGURE 11: New Order Army Regulars Buluks: Company Officer – Moulazeem: Lieutenant (1798).
FIGURE 12: Uskudar Regiment Soldier and their riding horse (1802).

C.Flaherty

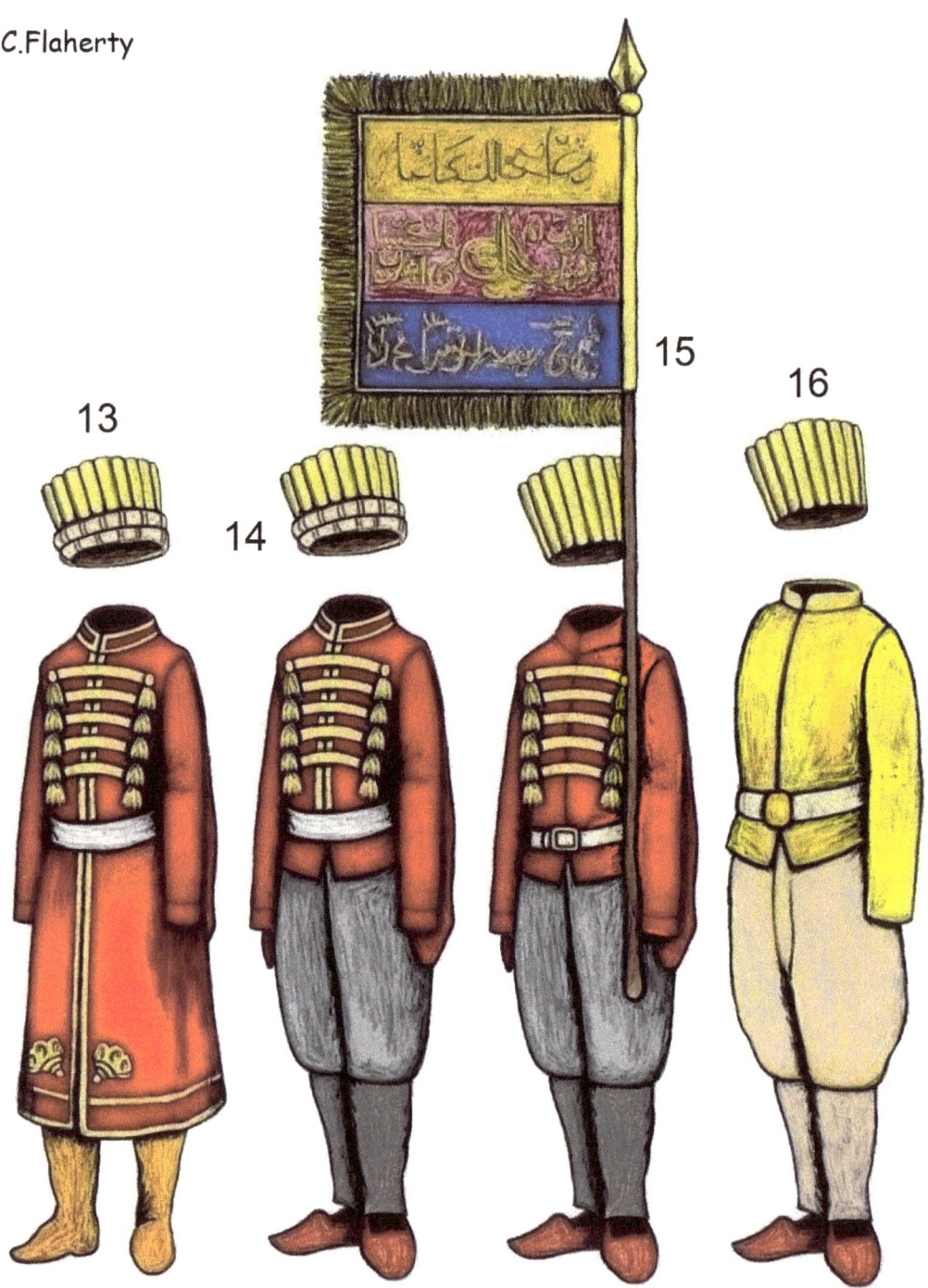

FIGURE 13: Bimbashi: Chef de Bataillon, up till 1810.
FIGURE 14: Yuzbasi: Captain or Buluks: Company Commander, up till 1810.
FIGURE 15: Moulazeem: Buluks: Company Lieutenant, up till 1810. This figure is carrying a New Order Army Regimental standard from the Sultan Selim III Era.
FIGURE 16: Sultan's Household Infantry Soldier, up till 1810.

CHAPTER 2: OFFICERS' RANKS AND INSIGNIA

Rank in the New Order Army was shown in two ways: "The main difference between the uniforms of the ... [Soldier] ... and the Officers were the swords and the buttons sewn above the pockets of the latter."[67] An illustration described in French as: "Regne du Sultan Abdul ... [Mahmud II] ... Avan l'Introduction de l'Uniforme Europeenn": before the introduction of the European uniform[68], shows a Senior Officer in a long coat. The rank grade is indicated with yellow chest tape and tassels, and collar piping. In error, the original figure is identified as a Kol Achassi: Adjutant-Major (in reference to a later 1876 till 1908 rank). The 1907 error in the book text, was to use post-1876 Turkish Army ranks. The Bimbashi: Major - Chef de Bataillon was assumed to have been a Full-Colonel (later 1876 till 1908 rank of Miralay). Other figures, in error, were given corresponding lower grade Officer ranks. The correct 1798 till 1807 system of ranks:

Chef de Bataillon	Equated to a Bimbashi: Major
Yuzbasi	Captain or Buluks: Company Commander
Moulazeem	Buluks: Company Lieutenant

1798 PAMPHLET NEW ORDER ARMY OFFICER RANKS

The 1798 Pamphlet illustration and description of New Order Army Officer ranks show the following distinctions, that consisted of large domed chest buttons used in pairs[69]:

RANK	CHEST CORDS OR BUTTONS	RANK	CHEST BUTTONS
1. Colonel	Nine Chest Cords	5. Lieutenant	Four Pairs
2. Lieutenant-Colonel	Five Pairs	6. Sous Lieutenant	Three Pairs
3. Adjudant-Major	Four Pairs	7. Porte Drapeau	Two Pairs
4. Capitaine	Four Pairs	8. Sergent-Major	One Pair

The 1798 New Order Army Colonel wore a long coat closed at the front by chest cords that button in the center, and had tasseled ends. An 1850 illustration of a Yuzbachi [Yuzbasi], Capitaine d'Infanterie, Infantry Captain, or Buluks: Company Commander, up till 1810[70], is depicted wearing a tall red bonnet with a blue top tuft, with a yellow turban wrapped around the base. A collarless buttoned white shirt is worn with a long red collarless robe-coat with long open sleeves, and this displays a pair of enormous chest buttons with sunburst edges, and center knobs, with chains hanging. It is known, that large, patterned metal chest buttons, appeared each side of Janissary long coats, used by Cuisinier Janissaire: Janissary Cook [Corbaci]: Orta Colonels[71].

TRANSITION FROM FRENCH TO TURKISH RANKS

A key issue to consider, the 1798 Pamphlet covering New Order Army Officer ranks, were those directly taken from the French Army, and very rapidly within a year the more familiar Turkish equivalent ranks – some of which have origins in the Janissary come into general usage, and this transformation leads to an adjustment in uniforms and rank insignia, in two phases:

67	Shaw, 1965.
68	Sevket, 1907.
69	Raif, 1798.
70	Brindesi, 1850.
71	Sevket, 1907.

FRENCH RANK	TURKISH RANK	COAT TYPE WITH CORDS OR CHEST BUTTONS	
		First Phase	Second Phase
Colonel	Aga	Long fur edged coat	Nine Cords
Lieutenant-Colonel	Bimbashi	Long gold embroidered coat	Five Pairs
Adjutant-Major	Aga-yi Yemen (Major of the Right) Aga-yi Yesar (Major of the Left)		Four Pairs
JUNIOR OFFICERS		Short Jacket	
Capitaine	Yuzbasi	Four Pairs	Four Pairs
Lieutenant	Moulazeem	Three Pairs	Four Pairs
Sous-Lieutenant			Three Pairs*
Porte Drapeau:	Alemdar: Flag Bearer	Three Pairs	Two Pairs
Sergeant-Major	Cavus	Two Pairs	One Pair
Corporal	Odabasi	One Pair	NONE

*Moulazeem ranks expand to include a Senior, and Junior Officer. Later known in the Turkish Army as the Mulazim-i-Evvel: Full-Lieutenant, and Mulazim-i-Sani: Lieutenant.

In the case of the Levend Chiftlik Regiment, at Acre landing (in 1799), its Colonel–Commander was Sir Sydney Smith, and Lieutenant-Colonel was Aga [Agha] Soliman [Solyman]. Aga were normally high-ranking Ottoman Officials, usually wearing long fur edged coats typical of their status. Later representations of two Senior Boustangees' Officers, show a distinct rank system distinguishing the two from each other, as one display four, and the other seven (that can be seen) embroidered chest bars ending in tassels – indicating one is a higher rank than the other. The other significant issue is the 1798 Pamphlet description did not include the rank of Odabasi: Corporal, who was to become identified with one pair of chest buttons – that became so for the 1826 Mansure Army, under Sultan Mahmud II. Adding the Odabasi: Corporal, under the Cavus: Sergeant-Major, effectively caused all the other ranks above to go up, and extra pair of button insignia.

ALEMDAR: FLAG BEARER

Each New Order Army Buluks: Company had an Alemdar: Flag Bearer [72]. A 1798 Pamphlet illustration shows a figure of a New Order Army Officer carrying a flag as one of the Battalion Staff[73]. Like the other Officers, wears a jersey-jacket with low standing collar, decorated with tape bars. The 1798 Pamphlet illustration shows all the Officers wearing over their jersey-jackets a long loose collarless coat, open at the front, with wide sleeves. The Alemdar displays two pairs of chest buttons. Wide waist sash with Russian pants, and Turkish riding boots complete the dress.

NEW ORDER ARMY REGIMENT FLAGS

A 1798 Pamphlet illustration of a New Order Army flag[74], shows this to be a small rectangular one, displaying a plain field, likely to have been plain green or red, which also may indicate (as the illustration is not very clear) some type of tape edge, or fringe is used. It should also be noted that many Janissary flags used a broad yellow border[75]. A short pole topped with a ball and small upwards-pointing crescent finial is carried. A surviving flag assumed to be a New Order Army Regimental standard from the Sultan Selim III Era[76], is quite distinctive as it consists of three horizontal bands: yellow (at the top), blue and red – not unlike common Janissary and Foot Soldier Officer's Command Flags used at the same time. It has gold fringes, and covered with lines of gold Ottoman script, and the Sultan's Tugra: signature.

72   Shaw, 1965.
73   Raif, 1798.
74   Raif, 1798.
75   Sevket, 1907.
76   Askeri Muze.

CHAPTER 3: GENERALSHIP AND OFFICERS' COMMAND

The New Order Army focused on Soldier, and reform of the Kapikulu Ocaklari: Standing Army, and as one 1770s Turkish Military Official complained: "contrasting Ottoman disorder to the regimental order of the Christians, who had become like a string of camels reined in and led by a camel driver." [77] However, there was also another problem, the general historical consensus is that Turkish Generals were incapable of managing field armies tactically[78]. Historians generally view there was, "retention of ... [a] ... tactical system ... introduced in the 16th and 17th Centuries signaled a self-destructive adherence to conservative military tradition."[79] Turkish Generals usually moved their armies into battle in a disconnected and piecemeal deployment. This practice was intentional as the Turkish Army traditionally marched onto an intended battlefield, rather in the manner of a, "pageant-like review of the Cavalry and Infantry ... before the Sultan or Commander."[80] Inability to coordinate, was a key problem in Turkish grand battle tactics, so much so, it was advised by a German commentator, in the Napoleonic Period: "Partial engagements should be avoided, because in these the Turks are superior; whereas they are quite ignorant of the art of fighting in mass, and with unity of object."[81]

Inability to coordinate may have been due to language problems and communications. A 1770s Turkish Military Official complained Arnaut: Albanian Irregulars, "would obey no one ... spoke Albanian among themselves, and did not understand Turkish[82]. The Turkish Army was itself a 'polyglot' assembled of various nations with different cultures, dress, language etcetera[83]. Turkish Generalship was said to have shown an inability to coordinate its forces, which was the basis of this criticism made of the uprising to dislodge the French Siege of Acre, namely the local Turkish resistance was, "unacquainted with the nature of combined movements, were astonished to find themselves beaten at the same moment along a line of twenty-seven miles by an inferior body of the French."[84]

GRAND VIZIER'S COMMAND, CONTROL AND MILITARY COMPETENCY

A 1789 account of the Russian-Turkish War tells of the Grand Vizier, Jussuf Bacha who, "was occupied in forming the plan of an attack, which he meditated against the Austrians"[85]. In terms of direct battle control, it is known when the French advance at Heliopolis caused a rout the, "Grand Vizier, at the head of his attendants, endeavored more than once, but in vain, to rally this dastardly rabble."[86] Prior to that rout, "the Grand Vizier no sooner saw his advanced guard destroyed, than he moved forward with his whole Army to avenge their loss."[87] These examples show the Grand Vizier at key moments directly ordering his Soldiers into an attack, as well as attempting to rally them.

The military competency of 18th Century Turkish Generals, are known from some accounts, for instance in 1772, responding to the disorder of his Artillery, the Grand Vizier Muhsinzade Mehmed ordered a training exercise:

77	Aksan, 2007.
78	Reid, 2000.
79	Reid, 2000.
80	Reid, 2000.
81	Valentini, 1828.
82	Aksan, 2007.
83	Morier, 1801.
84	Camden, 1814.
85	Anthing, 1813.
86	Morier, 1801.
87	Alison, 1842.

"After the Gunners, equipped with ill-processed gunpowder and ill-mounted …[cannon] … failed in three attempts to hit their target, they succeeded at the fourth attempt and were suitably rewarded. The Grand Vizier ordered daily practice, which he supervised himself now and then, and in time, the Gunners became proficient at rapid-fire target and mortar fire, Master Gunners emerged from among the novices, and the Regiment's morale improved."[88]

An 1800 account from the Egyptian campaign, by a British Royal Navy Officer attached to his Staff, compared the Turkish Grand Bashaw [Pasha]: the Admiral and General in Egypt, "a more useful man for the service than the Great Turk … [the Grand Vizier]."[89] Another English account, from the diplomat who accompanied Yousuf Pasha, the Grand Vizier, in Egypt, described him, "[as] … of a mild disposition, but of a weak and irresolute character."[90] It was further noted that as a, "General, his … [military] … knowledge … can be but limited."[91] A key weakness in military decision making on campaign, or during a battle, was that much of it was decided in council. In Egypt, in 1800 where the Grand Vizier, was not militarily capable:

"For although the Grand Vizier represents the Sultan, and is alone entrusted with the supreme power, whether civil, military, or political, the Ministers are often called upon to decide a military question, which the energy of one man would carry into execution, but which they thwart often through timidity … ignorance, and sometimes through a spirit of opposition … The baneful effects of such mal administration are more severely felt when the irresolute disposition of a Vizier lays him open to their intrigues."[92]

In the case of the Egyptian campaign, in 1800, the Commissary General, a key advisor to the Grand Vizier, was decried by a commentator as, "never was an Army more ill appointed than this."[93] Not all Generals in the 18th Century, were seen as militarily poorly qualified. For instance, in the opening maneuvers, at the Battle of Forhani, in 1789 during a Cavalry encounter, it was stated:

"In this battle the Turks lost six hundred … among whom were a great many Officers. They were commanded by Osmau … [Pasha] … one of their best Generals."[94]

Some Senior Commanders' behavior during battle appears to have been almost oblivious to events. During a naval battle between the Badere Zaffere, a Turkish 50-gun ship, and the HMS Seahorse, a 38-gun Artois-class fifth-rate frigate (fought on 6 July 1808), the Seahorse quickly disabled the Badere Zaffere, and continued to cannonade for several hours killing or wounding most of the Turkish crew,

"then it was only by force … [from the other Officers] … that the Captain (who during the whole of the action had sat on the stern smoking his pipe) was prevented from blowing her up, whilst the Officers caused her colors to be struck."[95]

The second account of an oblivious commander smoking his pipe, is from the Battle of Heliopolis in 1800, where a disaster quickly unfolded, and a massive rout ensued. As the victorious French advanced:

"to cut-off his retreat … [the Turkish Commander] … permitted to approach within a mile of him, mistaking them for his own troops; and it was not till Captain Lacy, of the Engineers, (who had reconnoitered the enemy) apprised him of his danger, that he could be persuaded to rise from his sofa, and leave his pipe."[96]

88	Aksan, 2002.
89	Low, 1911.
90	Morier, 1801.
91	Morier, 1801.
92	Morier, 1801.
93	Morier, 1801.
94	Anthing, 1813.
95	McLean, 1818.
96	Morier, 1801.

Interestingly, an 1827 (till 1830) painting of a Turkish fortress wall Battery at Pylos, during the Battle of Navarino[97], shows the Battery Commander sitting still on a raised viewing platform, while the rest of the gun crews and Officers are highly animated.

JANISSARY OFFICERS' COMMAND AUTHORITY

The critical flaw in Infantry organization was the lack of effective leadership, and piecemeal approach to conventional battle. The Turkish Army by the late-18th Century was based on an ethos of individual valor. It was often commented how 'Soldiers fought as individuals rather than as organized Battalions'[98]. Compared to European armies, which had adopted a universal system of graded Non-Commissioned Officers and Officers, by the end of the 17th Century ensuring a high level of command and control, Turkish on the other hand had very few Officers to lead their Soldiers. Commonly there was a Commander of an Orta, or Campaign Regiment, and several Officers to lead units that consisted of a thousand or more.

Janissary disciplinary rules established by Sultan Murad I (1362 to 1389), called for, "total obedience to Officers"; and, "punishment by only their own Officers"[99]. Notwithstanding, Janissary Officers appear to have traditionally had very little in the way of actual command authority, as this might be understood in modern terms, or even as the concept developed in the 18th Century. What they possessed was social status:

> "Officers below the Colonel carries none of that respectability which is attached to the same rank in our Armies: the Ensign and Captain attend upon the Colonel as menial servants; I have seen them wait at his table, and stand before him in the attitude that denotes the widest difference of rank in life."[100]

While this may seem odd, to modern eyes, an Officer, even if only serving, was at the table - so to speak, in a position to influence. It was a significant ritual event:

> "Such a formation acted throughout as both magnet and focus of kinship. The ceremonial meal with Commanders and Senior Officials, and the ... [Janissary] ... at headquarters the night before battle, was emblematic of the paternal relationship"[101].

JANISSARY INDIVIDUALITY

The Janissary Orta: Battalion represented a brotherhood of trained full-time paid Soldiers. Traditionally, highly skilled bowmen, swordsmen and later musketeers operated as individuals collectively attacking a target, effectively swarming around their enemy. Their rough-order battle formations reflected the basic Janissary combat ethos: "every individual Turkish Soldier imagines himself opposed singly to the enemy's Army"[102]. The lack of control exercised by Officers, meant that individually Janissary made their own decision to fight or not: "he feels the impossibility of resisting it, and thinks it but reason able that he should retire."[103]

NUMBER OF AVAILABLE JANISSARY OFFICERS

It is likely, that the number of Janissary Officers in any of the Orta: Battalion was not set. Appointments were based on seniority, not on the organizational numbers present,

> "The Junior Officers, namely ... [the Odabasi] ... were appointed according to their experience and

---

97	Garneray, 1827.
98	Valentini, 1828.
99	Nicolle, 1995.
100	Morier, 1801.
101	Aksan, 2002.
102	Morier, 1801.
103	Morier, 1801.

influence in their Regiments and they were in close contact with the rank-and-file Janissary in their daily life. It was these Officers rather than the … [Corbaci] … Commanding Officers of the Janissary … [Orta: Battalions] … or the higher echelons of the Janissary Command who better understood and represented the interests of rank-and-file Janissary. Although these Officers usually came from the lower classes, they held significant political power with their capacity to control the rank-and-file Janissary."[104]

The lack of available Junior Officers was recognized around the 1740s[105]. Military reforms attempted to redress the problem, albeit without success. It was proposed to reorganize Janissary Orta: Battalions into smaller tactical units, and increase the number of Junior Officers to create better battlefield maneuverability.

ACTUAL CONTROL AUTHORITY

In the case of the Janissary Officer, it was likely that they had very little actual control authority, for instance in this account from Egypt, in 1800, where in response to Soldiers wildly firing their muskets at night:

> "The Grand Vizier sent an Officer to them with orders to desist; but no sooner had those orders reached them, than it was a signal for increasing their fire"[106].

Even though the Janissary may have appeared to have little command sway, there was still at the same time a high level of discipline maintained, as can be seen in one episode of two Janissary, "who were strangled for outrages of … [plundering] … the poor Arabs that came to sell their vegetables and milk."[107] This occurred as the Turkish Army marched into Egypt, in 1800. In this case, it seems likely, the explanation for the severity of the penalty was breaking the law – the robbery of people providing for the Army while on the march, which was a key part of the supply and logistics strategy.

NEW ORDER ARMY OFFICERS' COMMAND AUTHORITY

The key reform of the New Order Army was to introduce an actual system of command and control. Introduction of a set number of Officers with an actual corresponding number of Soldiers they controlled. New Order Army Officers exercised a different level of command role in relation to their Soldiers, compared to that exercised by their Janissary counterparts. For instance, it is known that Soldiers in the new Corps complained how their, "work was too hard … [and] … the discipline too severe"[108].

One problem affecting the command role of New Order Army Officers was the massive disproportion of Soldiers' numbers to the few Officers enrolled[109]. The lack of available Officers meant that less than a fifth of the number needed to fill the basic organizational structure for a New Order Army Regiment of some 64 field Officers (of various grades), and 1,080 Soldiers, or one Officer per 17 Soldiers approximately, was not met. As recruitment and training of New Order Army Regulars grew in number from 1797 till 1801, the problem only became more severe:

May, 1797	2,536 Soldiers	27 Officers	One Officer for every 93 Soldiers
September, 1799	4,317 Soldiers	30 Officers	One Officer for every 144 Soldiers
April, 1800	6,029 Soldiers	27 Officers	One Officer for every 223 Soldiers
July, 1801	9,263 Soldiers	27 Officers	One Officer for every 343 Soldiers

104 Sunar, 2006.
105 Levy, 1982.
106 Morier, 1801.
107 Morier, 1801.
108 Shaw, 1965.
109 Shaw, 1965.

By 1806, the relationship of Officers to Soldiers had improved dramatically, as the New Order Army had 22,685 Soldiers and 1,590 Officers[110][111]. Representing one Officer for every 14 Soldiers.

ORIGIN OF OFFICERS IN THE NEW ORDER ARMY

The origin of the Turkish Officers recruited to join the New Order Army from 1797 till 1801, and those added to the ranks of this organization following 1800, and until 1807, are known to have come from the ranks: "Their Officers are all Turks, and are chosen out of those who perform their exercise the best."[112] Officers were annually promoted:

> "A regular hierarchy of promotion was established within the corps, with vacancies filled by the persons occupying the posts immediately beneath them and everyone else moving up one notch. However, provision was made for the advancement of unusually qualified men out of order in special cases, especially if they showed their ability in battle. Among persons of equal ability, however, preference had to be given to age and seniority."[113]

NEW ORDER ARMY JUNIOR OFFICERS

The organization of the New Order Army co-opted terms such as Cavus: "Sergeant or Disciplinary Officer"[114][115]. The Cavus had generally been a Janissary title; in the New Order Army the rank was reconstituted as a European-styled rank conforming to a Senior Non-Commissioned Officer. Even the Odabasi: Janissary Barrack-Room Chief became the New Order Army Corporal[116]. The origin of the New Order Army Cavus, and Odabasi were likely selected from the Soldiers who successfully passed training. It is also possible these Junior Officers were one source for some Senior Grade Officers selection[117].

ROLE OF EUROPEAN OFFICERS AND TRAINERS

Arriving with the Turkish Army which had invaded Egypt, an English journal account recalls seeing, "some of our Artillerymen who had been at Constantinople instructing the Turks appeared here like gentlemen."[118] At an encounter between French Soldiers, in Egypt, and Turkish force under the command of two British Officers - Colonel Hope, an Artillery Officer, and Major Holloway,

> "brought up the Turkish Artillery and Infantry to the fight in a wood of date trees, where the superiority of European discipline was not so decisive as in the open plain, while a skillful movement of the Cavalry towards ... [the French Army's] ... rear threatened to cut-off the enemy's retreat to Cairo."[119]

During the Egyptian campaign, it is known that various British Officers partnered with Turkish Commanders. For instance, in one battle between Turkish and the retreating French Army – "On this occasion Colonel Holloway and Major Hope acted with the Vizier, Captain Lacey with Mahomed … [Pasha] …. and Captain Leake with Taher … [Pasha]."[120]

The first recorded use of New Order Army Regulars was the arrival of the Levend Chiftlik Regiment at the 1799 Siege of Acre at Gaza, this coincided with the French Mission in Constantinople side-

---

110	Shaw, 1965.
111	Aksan, 2007.
112	Eton, 1798.
113	Shaw, 1965.
114	Shaw, 1965.
115	Nicolle, 1998.
116	Shaw, 1965.
117	Nicolle, 1998.
118	Low, 1911.
119	Alison, 1842.
120	Wittman, 1803.

lined, due to the French invasion of Egypt under Napoleon (with the end of the Franco-Ottoman Alliance in 1798)[121]. The British in support of the Sultans' rights to Egypt appears to have led to the situation where command of the New Order Army Battalion, was given to Sir Sydney Smith:

> "introducing the Levend Chiftlik Regiment … disciplined after the European method under Sultan Selim's own eye, and placed, by His Imperial Majesty's express command, as my … [Sir Sydney Smith] … disposal."[122]

Even though Command went to Sir Sydney Smith, there was also a Turkish Colonel–Commander of the Levend Chiftlik Regiment, at the Acre landing. This was its Lieutenant-Colonel Soliman [Solyman] Aga [Agha][123][124][125]. Suggesting a command pairing of the two Officers, which may have been a widespread practice.

OFFICER'S COMMAND FLAGS

An 1801 account about the Sipahi: Cavalry flags, referring to the summoning of the Regiment, that they, "have their Officers … are obliged to assemble, properly armed and equipped, on the first summons, under the colours of their district … [Sanjakbeg: Governor]."[126][127] At the battle of Heliopolis in Egypt, when the Sipahi: Cavalry were making ready to charge, "the concentration of their standards along their whole line gave the French warning that it was approaching"[128]. By the late-18th Century, and well into the Napoleonic Period, all Infantry and Cavalry Officers carried their own Command Flags.

The 1810 Sultan Mahmud II Grand Review shows a Janissary Musketeer Regiment with an Officer carrying a large square flag with three horizontal bars, each cut into a pointed tail, with a finial consisting of a crescent mounted on a ball[129]. Depicted with yellow, red, and yellow horizontal bars. Rather than being specific unit or organizational flags, many of the flags seen illustrated were more likely individual Commanding Officer's flags; either carried by the Officer themselves or by a personal attendant:

> "Turkish standards are large, particularly that which … denominated the … [Pasha] … as well as a great number of small flags or banderols belonging to the different corps. Each Troop consisting of twenty-five or thirty … having one"[130].

An English account from Egypt, in 1800 provides a description of the use of Musketeer, or Orta: Battalion Officers' Command Flags:

> "The Turks formed … their Officers or Standard Bearers running to the front with the flags and holding them up, their front line formed upon them and discharged their muskets, then the flags started to the front again, and so on."[131]

It is known, that every Officer had their own personal flag:

121	Shaw, 1965.
122	Howard, 1839.
123	Dodsley, 1801.
124	Camden, 1814.
125	Shaw, 1965.
126	Olivier, 1801.
127	Dalvimart, 1802.
128	Alison, 1842.
129	Unknown, 1810.
130	McLean, 1818.
131	Low, 1911.

"Every village, from which the Aga ... (a sort of Mayor) takes the field, may unfurl its particular standard. Hence it is that the capture of hundreds of such colors forms, but an insignificant trophy"[132].

A 1773 Russian-Turkish War account, noted during a massed Turkish Infantry attack:

"The Turks commenced the attack with a discharge of artillery; and immediately advanced against the ... [Russian entrenchments] ... with such ... [vigor] ... they continued to advance, and passed, in great numbers, over the chevaux-de-frise to the ... [palisades] ... where they fixed their standards"[133].

In Egypt in 1800, an English observer noted, "each of the small Companies, consisting of from twenty-five to thirty Privates, belonging to the corps of Infantry, carries a small flag or banderole."[134]

▼ Janissary Orta: Battalion Officer's and Sipahi: Cavalry Officer's Command Flags. The crescent finial is shown in detail.

132 Valentini, 1828.
133 Anthing, 1813.
134 Wittman, 1803.

CHAPTER 4: STANDING ARMY'S TACTICS

The Kapikulu Ocaklari: Standing Army, also known as Kapikulu Akerleri: Sultan's Army during the 15th to 17th Centuries[135], had by the French Revolution and later Napoleonic Wars changed little from the previous century[136]. One mid-18th Century Turkish military reformer, known as Gazi Hassan[137][138], advocated dividing, "the Army of 100,000 men into ten different Corps, which were to attack separately, and so arranged that the retreat of the repulsed Corps should not overwhelm and put in disorder those which had not attacked."[139] One of the initial reform proposals, following Sultan Selim III's accession, came from Tatarcikzade Abdullah, who wanted to make retrained Orta: Battalions of Musketeers, assigned with two to four rapid-fire cannons, manned by ten Sur'atcis [Suratci Ocagi]: Rapid-Fire Artillery Soldiers as the basic battlefield tactical unit[140]. The only major change to occur was introduction of a New Order Army Soldiers' Drill Manual, introducing Motions, contained in the 1798 Pamphlet[141]:

1. Portez vos Armes: Carry your weapon.	17. Appretez vos Armes: Prepare your weapon.
2. Par le Flanc Droit: By the right flank.	18. Joue: Cheek (rest weapon close to the cheek while firing – aiming it).
3. Par le Flanc Gauche: By the left flank.	19. Feu: Fire (level the weapon – fire without aiming).
4. Demi Tour: Half turn.	20. l'Arme au Bras: Cradle your weapon in the right arm.
5. En Avant Marche: Forward march.	21. Presentez vos Armes: Present your weapon.
6. Chargez vos Armes: Load your weapon.	22. l'Arme Sous le Bras Gauche: Reverse-holding weapon behind the left arm.
7. Prenez la Cartouche: Take the cartridge.	23. A Genoux: On your knees presenting your weapon.
8. Dechirez la Cartouche: Tear the cartridge.	24. Reposez-vous sur vosArmes: Lower your weapon down your right hand (butt resting on the ground).
9. Amorcez: Prime.	25. Vos Armes a Terre: Your weapon on the ground.
10. Fermez le Bassinet: Close the lock.	26. l'Arme a Droite: Hold the weapon on the right.
11. l'Arme a Gauche: Weapon down to the left.	27. Otez la Bayonnette: Take off the bayonet.
12. Cartouche au Canon: Load the remaining cartridge.	28. Remettez la Bayonnette: Put back the bayonet.
13. Tirez la Baguette: Pull the ramrod out.	29. La Bayonnette vers l'Ennemi Fantasin: Bayonet towards enemy Infantry.
14. Bourrez: Insert ramrod in muzzle.	30. Croisez la Bayonnette vers l'Ennemi Cavalier: Cross the bayonet towards enemy Cavalry.
15. Remettez la Baguette: Return the ramrod.	31. Signal: Raise your right hand to signal.
16. Portez vos Armes: Carry your weapon.	32. Descendez vos Armes et Marchez: Hold weapon low by the right side and walk.

The 1798 Pamphlet also shows the camp was still important, as it was to Janissary battles when an entrenched camp was established for the Infantry and Artillery to fight from, to New Order Army's deployment for battle[142]. The New Order Army's camp was laid-out in ordered bands (Janissary camps were irregular), with Senior Officer's tents in the rear. Before the Officer's tents were set up large cooking pots. In front of the cooking pots was the Soldier's tent blocks, arranged in two in-

---
135 Nicolle, 1995.
136 Valentini, 1828.
137 Eton, 1798.
138 Shaw, 1965.
139 Eton, 1798.
140 Aksan, 2007.
141 Raif, 1798.
142 Raif, 1798.

wards facing lines of eight tents (totalling 16 tents in each block). There were six tent blocks. Before each line of tents a limbered cannon was set up (some 12 cannons in a line). In front, Soldiers are lined-up in blocks 11 lines deep, and 22 files across (some 242 Soldiers estimated in each Infantry block), with bayonets at the ready. Ten Infantry blocks are depicted, each with a banner. It can therefore be estimated, there are some 2,420 in the entire formation.

The 1798 Pamphlet illustration of these larger Infantry blocks of 242 Soldiers is more than the equivalent of two Buluks: Companies, composed of 90 Soldiers and 10 Officers each; and is at variance with the New Order Army Infantry Regiment that was set at 1,600 Soldiers and Officers, divided into Sub-Divisions of 800 supported by five light cannon handled by Soldiers in close support, as the basic battlefield tactical unit.

▼ Three possible tactical deployment options for New Order Army Regiment's Sub-Divisions of six Buluks: Companies, with their supporting cannon: (A) Column attack formation with Buluks: Companies' cannons massed creating a fire corridor. (B) Line-cannon attack formation with each Buluks: Company cannon handled forward, as Infantry behind advance. (C) Defensive line formation, with Buluks: Companies' cannons massed on higher ground behind the Infantry.

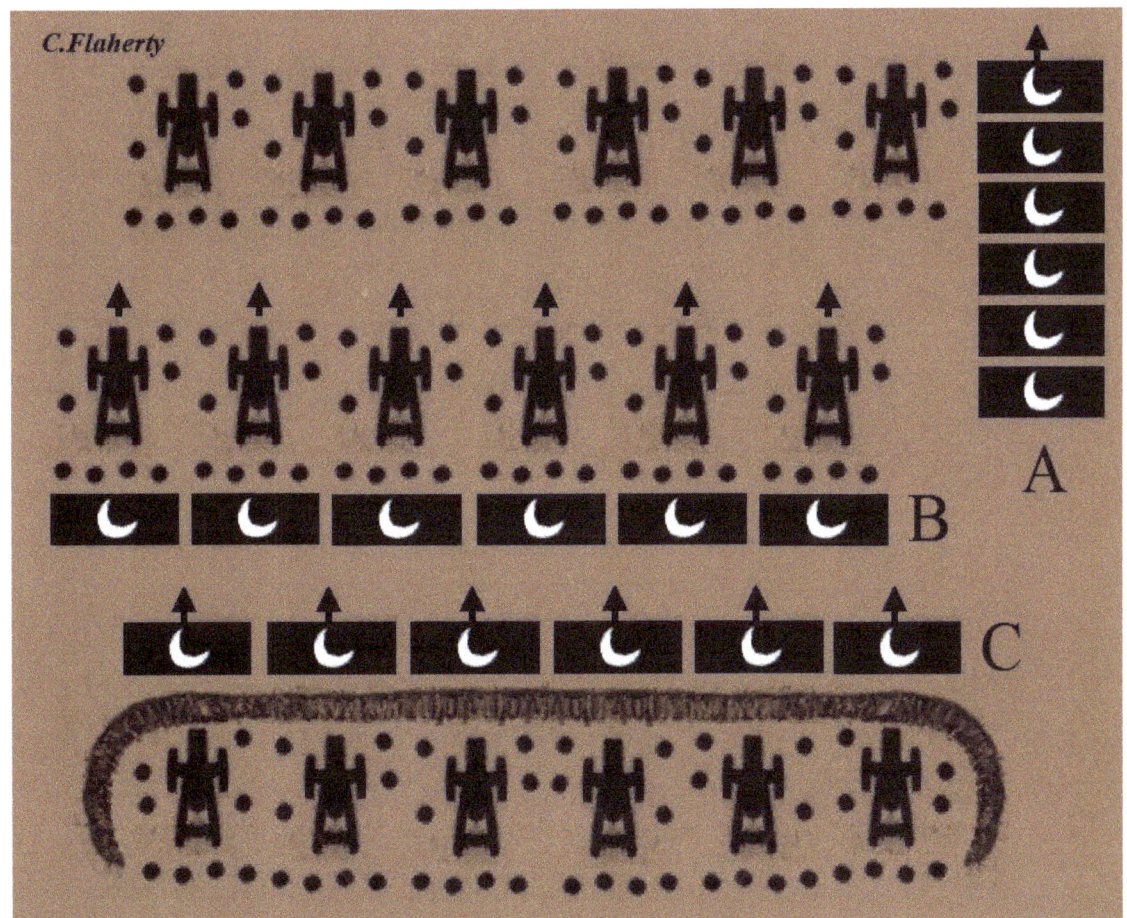

TABUR-CENGI: DEFENSIVE FORMATION

Significantly, the New Order Army Regulars' camp hearken back to older Turkish Army grand battle tactics based on Tabur-Cengi: Defensive Formation and 18th Century Entrenchment Battles. Several illustrations from 1732, show large-scale aerial views of the Turkish Army deployed for battle[143]. In contrast to opposing European Imperial Battalions, the Turkish Army is shown swarming out from its encampment, forming into a massed semi-circular formation. Prior to 18th Century practice of the Army swarming from their entrenchments, the Turkish Tabur-Cengi: defensive formation was the predominant battle-tactic used. It had emerged during the 15th to 17th Centuries:

"[as] … an effective counter to … Western Pike … and Musketeer formations. Tactically it was a static formation, which invited an enemy attack. From the end of the 15th Century, most European Armies had adopted the use of the pike often in conjunction with firearms, forming mixed units of … [Pike Soldiers] … and Musketeers. Whereas … [Turkish Soldiers] … tended to adopt purely musket and bow armed units alone supported by Artillery … The … [Turkish] … tactically speaking saw musketry, supported by Light Artillery as well as bow armed troops as sufficiently capable of destroying an attack with firepower alone."[144]

▲ Arabaci: Transport Corps wagon pushed into position for a Tabur-Cengi: defensive formation and mounted with Janissary, using wooden shields for added protection.

---

143   Marsigli, 1732.
144   Mugnai, 2015.

Arabaci: Transport Corps wagon, used for transport, cannon limber and mobile fortification, played a central role in forming the Tabur-Cengi: defensive formation. Modern history accounts state the design of Arabaci wagons are missing[145]. However, a wagon is depicted in a 1596 Ottoman miniature of the Battle of Keresztes[146]. The wagon has four large similarly sized wheels[147], with high wooden sides, and with heavy round wood shields attached. The wagons are lined-up, and chained together, with Artillery placed in front creating a defensive position. Janissary and other Foot Soldiers armed with bows, heavy arquebuses and muskets shield the Cannoneers. More Janissary were arranged, commonly, "[in] … several rows deep … [and] … remained within the formation."[148] The rear and wings were secured by Sipahi: Cavalry. At the battle of Mohacs (29 August 1526), the Tabur-Cengi: defensive formation used 150 wagons and 4,000 Janissary in nine rows, with Artillery in the center firing at close quarters[149].

ENTRENCHMENT BATTLES

"The manner in which the Turks carry on their operations, in conformity with their cautious system, is as follows: they select upon the road, along which they wish to advance, an advantageous post, and entrench themselves; then they call in reinforcements, and wait to be attacked. If they are not attacked, they advance again, after a lapse of time, to another favorable post, which they never fail to entrench, even though they should only occupy it for one night. But they remain for days, and even weeks, in deliberation whether to advance further. If, however, time is allowed them, they are sure to approach so near, and place themselves in such a manner, as to offer considerable annoyance, and we are finally compelled to attack them in their own entrenchments."[150]

By the 18th Century, Tabur-Cengi: defensive formation had evolved into entrenched encampment at the center of an Army's deployment. At the Battle of Kartal, in 1770 the Russians reported how the Turkish Army,

"was arrayed in a crescent, with Anatolian Cavalry on the left flank, Rumelian … [Ottoman South-Eastern European] … Cavalry on the right, and the Tatars positioned in advance to operate as raiding parties. The Grand Vizier's huge, richly embroidered tent was pitched in the center … [the Janissary] … themselves at the heart of the camp"[151].

Traditionally Janissary set up their tents, adjacent to the trenches they were occupying[152]. One particularly odd practice by a Janissary Orta: Battalion, who likely erected a highly decorated pavilion-tent as its insignia, was known to have taken,

"[a] … handful of younger Soldiers dressed as women … placed in a separate tent … called the Harem … and given a special Guard. They served as a sort of Regimental talisman and would be defended to the death in case of defeat."[153]

A 1787 account of the Russian-Turkish War: "The Turks were no sooner disembarked, than they began to form … [entrenchments]"[154]. By the late-18th Century, the Turkish Army developed entrenchment warfare, as the basis of their Grand Army Tactics:

"They constantly fortify their camps; and, when the day of battle arrives, draw out their forces in regular array in front of their … [entrenchments] … where their stores, tents, ammunition, and riches are deposited."[155]

145	Uyar, 2009.
146	Topkapi, 1609.
147	Nicolle, 1995.
148	Uyar, 2009.
149	Uyar, 2009.
150	Valentini, 1828.
151	Aksan, 2002.
152	Sakul, 2013.
153	Nicolle, 1998.
154	Anthing, 1813.
155	Alison, 1840.

It is generally known that Turkish trench work was, "deeper and longer with curves rather than the standard European sharp angles ... [zigzag trenches]"[156]. Dug by the Janissary and specialist Legamdji: Miners and Sappers, it is likely Turkish Infantry carried a substantial number of digging tools, or that a large component of a field unit was in fact dedicated diggers. A 1787 account of the Russian-Turkish War reports Turkish Infantry while constructing their entrenchments encountered the problem of flooding, this meant that they could not sufficiently dig deep enough: "They, however, supplied this defect, by filling the sacks, with which they had the precaution to provide themselves, with sand, and they served as a rampart."[157] Well known in the 18th Century, was the technique called: "epaulement, in fortification, a side-work hastily thrown up, to cover canon or Soldiers. It is made ... of bags of earth"[158].

A 1721 painting showing Turkish fighting the Polish Army[159], illustrates Turkish Infantry firing from a trench dug into the ground. The trench appears deep and wide enough to give cover to the chest-height allowing two ranks of Infantry to stand-up to fire their muskets. This suggests a trench approximately 5 feet: 1.5 meters deep, and 6 feet 1.8 meters wide. Spoil from trench excavation was piled behind, creating a sconce: raised earthwork for Artillery (consisting of mortars-howitzers interspaced between two batteries of three, and four cannons). The sconce is possibly only 3 feet: 1 meter high, allowing cannons to fire-overhead, and Infantry in the trench to directly fire at approaching enemy troops. Cavalry forms a crescent formation covering the flanks of the Infantry trench, and Artillery. Cavalry also formed-up behind the Artillery emplacement.

▲ A Turkish sconce for Artillery, and trench for Infantry battle formation.

---

156   Sakul, 2013.
157   Anthing, 1813.
158   Chambers, 1728.
159   Cavuszade, 1721.

Wide Distribution of Forces

Entrenchment tactics used by Turkish Infantry, appear to have involved a wide distribution of their forces. For instance, at the Battle of Forhani, in 1789 the Austrian and Russian advancing Corps faced large-scale Sipahi: Cavalry attacks, of 15,000 and 20,000 from their left and right flanks, which were well ahead of the Turkish Infantry entrenchments[160]. The trench line itself was weak, said to be, "ill raised, and not strengthened with sufficient Artillery"[161]; a fact supported by the capture of only twelve pieces. Trenches protected the camp, which was described as, "very rich, and … [containing] … immense magazines."[162] Russian and Austrian forces, encountered to the rear of the main Turkish entrenched camp two fortified Convents. Saint Samuel contained, "a considerable magazine of provisions … [was positioned] … in the rear, at a small distance from the … [entrenchments]"[163]. While the other, "not far … [Saint] … John, in which also was a great magazine of provisions."[164] The Convents appear to have been held by 200 to 300 Soldiers each.

Turkish entrenchment tactics did not follow a set-piece battle layout, instead sending large tactical divisions ahead of the main entrenched Army camp. For instance, at the battle of Heliopolis, in Egypt the Grand Vizier's Advanced Guard, comprising a force of 6,000 hand-picked Janissary established their camp well away from the main Turkish Army camp in the neighborhood of El-Hanka [Belbeis][165]. Janissary, it is said: "[had] … thrown up some rude fortifications", at the village of Matarieh[166]; also called, "Matharieh"[167]. This camp, "had been entrenched and armed with sixteen pieces of Artillery"[168]; and contained, "ammunition, tents"[169]. To the right of the Janissary position, there was a 1,200 Mameluke Regiment of Ibrahim-bey deployed as far as the banks of the Nile.

In general terms, while Entrenchment Battles were the norm, a 1770s Russian-Turkish Wars account shows that in not all instances was the battle tactic used:

> "the Turkish Army immediately extended itself, and presented an uncommon spectacle. Accustomed as they were to fight in small, scattered bands, the Turks now ranged themselves in European order of battle, and formed themselves in regular lines … [Janissary] … with the Artillery, occupying the center, and the … [Sipahi] … Cavalry, taking post on the wings."[170]

PONTOON BRIDGE DEFENCES

Early exponents of pontoon bridge engineering, Turkish fortified camps made use of rivers and waterways to secure them. The fortified bridge-ends only appear within the camp itself, and do not appear to have been constructed at both ends, as is typically seen in a Tete de Pont. The Turkish version of these fortifications may have been intended as a last bastion for the defence of the camp, covering an escape route, from the camp in case of defeat. Allowing defenders to quickly destroy the pontoons, to stop an attacker following over the bridge, covering the main Army's escape. The defenders would likely have escaped by boat.

---

160 Anthing, 1813.
161 Anthing, 1813.
162 Anthing, 1813.
163 Anthing, 1813.
164 Anthing, 1813
165 Phillips, 1803.
166 Alison, 1842.
167 Phillips, 1803.
168 Phillips, 1803.
169 Alison, 1842.
170 Anthing, 1813.

VOLLEY FIRE

A 1792 parade display by Grand Vizier Yusuf Pasha for Sultan Selim III of Omar Aga's Company: Turkish Soldiers using Russian Infantry Drill, said he, "was so struck with the superiority of the massed firepower which it was able to assemble"[171]. Sultan Selim III, it is said:

> "instantly saw the superiority of their fire to that of the ordinary Turkish troops, and appreciated more than ever the advantages which the arms and discipline of his Christian enemies had long given them over Turkish troops"[172].

The New Order Army Soldiers' Drill Manual introduced 14 Motions, associated with Line Infantry volley fire. The main difference between late-18th Century established practice and Janissary volley fire techniques, was standing and reloading. Janissary volley fire techniques were established by the start of the Long War, in the 1600s[173]. It is known Janissary used volley fire by the 1590s, and by the 16th Century Janissary fired their weapons row-by-row[174]. This tactic has also been described as meeting an enemy attack, "firing in volleys by rotating the ranks."[175] The general view of volley fire use is somewhat contradicted, as it is stated of the Janissary, "[they] … never used musketry in massed volleys, relying instead on individual skills and marksmanship.[176] Eyewitness accounts from 1605, describe Janissary volley fire practice. The Orta: Battalion formation was drawn-up in three ranks; with each Soldier ready with the match-cord lit. Most illustrations traditionally show extra lit and smoldering match cord tied loosely around the left-arm or wrist[177]. The cycle of fire (likely over a minute – as this was the typical rate of reloading time), began with the first rank firing their weapons[178]. The first rank bends-down to reload, while the next rank fires, and they bend-down (reloading). The third rank then fires over the backs of the first two ranks bent-over in the process of reloading. After, the third rank has fired, the first rank stands again, and fires their weapons (with the back-third rank taking the time to reload). It has been calculated Janissary volley fire techniques allowed a minimum delivery of nearly 330 rounds per-rank, every 20 seconds; and approximately 1,000 rounds at their target every minute (assuming 1,000 Janissary are in the volley fire formation). The amount of weapons fire delivered by a Janissary Musketeer Orta: Battalion, and how long this firefight lasted is open to conjecture.

INFANTRY FORMATIONS

The general view of Turkish Infantry tactics was that only the New Order Army, "[who's] … training was based on French military manuals … [had] … Infantry drawn up in two or three lines to provide reserves and mutual support."[179] Nevertheless, an English account from Egypt, in 1800 provides a description of Janissary three-line Infantry formations and skirmish parties:

> "The Turks formed in three lines ... [and] ... advancing briskly on our left, their ... front line formed ... and discharged their muskets ... [a French attack forced back the front line] ... They fell back on their 2nd and 3rd lines when they all got into confusion"[180].

The general historical view, "we have very limited information about Janissary combat formations and how they actually fought"[181]. Janissary were renowned classically for their high levels of discipline, courage and training; in particular, "personal valor … had been a part of the Turkish military

---

171	Shaw, 1965.
172	Creasy, 1878.
173	Borekci, 2006.
174	Agoston, 2011.
175	Uyar, 2009.
176	Nicolle, 1995.
177	Knotel, 1890.
178	Borekci, 2006.
179	Nicolle, 1998.
180	Low, 1911.
181	Uyar, 2009.

ethos for centuries."[182] Only a few Junior Officers were available to lead an Orta: Battalion, and rather than rely on Officers leading, Janissary had a much greater capacity for self-organization. Tactically speaking this had some disadvantages, as Janissary attacks frequently, "disordered ... [the] ... crowd of Turks ... and ... the attack of that of the Turks ... returns to the charge as rapidly as it is dispersed."[183]

The 1798 Pamphlet shows New Order Army Infantry Soldiers formed in blocks 11 lines deep, and 22 files across (some 242 Soldiers estimated), with bayonets at the ready. Traditionally, the Janissary is known to have formed several rows deep within Tabur-Cengi: defensive formations. Illustrations of Turkish military formation from 1732, show the Janissary adopting one of two moving columns, one is two long files spaced apart, the other is four close parallel files; and this formation shows each row staggered, likely to allow two or several rows to face an enemy and fire at once[184]. Ottoman Court painting from the 16th Century often show the Janissary in line formations of two to three staggered ranks, allowing men at intervals to load, fire and reload simultaneously.

Janissary and other Foot Soldiers are shown in Ottoman Court paintings deployed in long lines directly behind a line of cannons firing over these. Some are deployed in long queues, and this may be representing tactics involving Turkish Infantry moving in column. Another formation shown are two long single-file columns of Janissary marching between cannons, for rapid deployment into a volley firing-line. These illustrations may indicate that Janissary and other Foot Soldiers were able to undertake column advances through the spaces, where they launched offensive sorties, between the individual cannon. This tends to show a high level of tactical sophistication, where the Artillery fire is used to bombard attacking forces, at longer range; giving Infantry opportunity to advance along fire corridors. Tactics such as these maximize the effect of cannon fire – keeping the advancing enemy under fire for as long as possible. Tactics, such as these would come to dominate the later Napoleonic battlefield. These tactics also compensated for the lack of firepower and limited range of muskets. Taking the offensive, the whole column could forge forward, in an all-out assault at full running speed when the enemy was within close-proximity, and had already lost coherent battle formation, having been continuously under fire from Artillery and small arms.

It is known, Janissary traditionally preferred deep formations deployed in several rows. These allowed them to achieve a continuous barrage of fire by rotating rows forward. This may refer to a column deployment between individual cannons. Shown to be several ranks deep in period illustrations. Janissary mainly employed deep formations only on the defensive, such as when they were deployed between the Artillery, protecting them. The key to these formations was deception:

> "Turks were cunning enough to make several false attacks, and to place considerable corps of reserve, one behind the other, which, suddenly checking the imprudent pursuit of the Christians, might drive them back, and penetrate into the openings of their lines."[185]

Skirmishing Tactics

It is known that a Turkish Infantry attack, "advanced in groups of 40 to 50, one rank or group advancing and firing while the second reloaded, maintaining their steady advance in the face of considerable losses."[186] In the Napoleonic Period, Janissary organization and tactics began to resemble the Light Infantry ethos: "Their discipline and mode of fighting was very similar to the English Light Infantry or French Tirailleurs."[187] It is known, some Janissary, were purposed in the Napoleonic Period as trained Light Infantry; namely, "39th Orta was designated as Light Infantry and the 44th Orta is known to have been deployed in skirmish order in several battles."[188] There is an earlier account from the 1770s Russian-Turkish Wars, which identifies the Janissary first, "advanced in

---

182	Buyukakca, 2007.
183	Valentini, 1828.
184	Marsigli, 1732.
185	Valentini, 1828.
186	Nicolle, 1998.
187	Alison, 1840.
188	Johnson, 1988.

skirmishing ... [and being] ... accustomed as they were to fight in small scattered bands"[189]. There is another 1770s reference to Turkish skirmish tactics, namely: "The Turkish Infantry posted themselves behind the hedges, where they did considerable mischief"[190]. Janissary, in the 18th Century, absorbed Rayas: Musketeer Sharp- Shooters. A peasant class in Ottoman Europe, who had become proficient huntsmen, were recruited as Auxiliaries and organized into Companies of 50 to 100 Soldiers. It is known, Rayas were rarely organized into larger units. Usually assigned to Janissary for use as skirmishers, and for other traditional Light Infantry duties[191]. At the Battle of Heliopolis, in Egypt, the French during their advance were attacked by Turkish, "Sharp-Shooters ... concealed in the wood."[192]

Circular Groups

It is possible, New Order Army Soldiers trained to form squares to repel Cavalry. Illustrations of Turkish military formation from 1732, show Janissary moving in small circular groups, each led by a flag bearer, with groups clustered in a checkerboard fashion[193]. Strictly speaking, Turkish Infantry did not practice forming square against Cavalry. Traditionally, Infantry entrenched as a defence, or were given close flanking cover by the Sipahi: Cavalry. Solak traditionally, when accompanying the Sultan into the field, practiced a surrounding formation where they completely encircled the Sultan covering him from attack. Personal Guards appear to use the same formation-maneuver. Use of spaced circular formations, appears to have led to Turkish commonly not adopting a formal battle front:

> "The presenting of a front, or the regular deployment of troops, was as little practiced among the Turks of that period as among those of the present day: they constantly brought forward contiguous swarms, which often entirely surrounded ... [their opponent] ... a mode of fighting which perhaps naturally resulted from their superiority in point of numbers, and from the general ardor with which this furious multitude rushed to the attack."[194]

MASS ATTACKS WITH THE KILIJ: SCIMITAR-SWORD

New Order Army Soldiers' Drill Manual, introduced two Motions, associated with bayonet fighting techniques: Motion 29: La Bayonnette vers l'Ennemi Fantassin: Bayonet towards enemy Infantry; and, Motion 30: Croisez la Bayonnette vers l'Ennemi Cavalier: Cross the bayonet towards enemy Cavalry. The general 18th Century opinion of Janissary hand-to-hand combat abilities, was:

> "In close or single combat, whether in the field or in the breach, the European bayonet has never proved a match for the Turkish ... [scimitar]"[195].

> "[Europeans] ... overpower us ... by the superiority of their fire, which, in fact, it is impossible to approach; but let them leave their abominable Batteries, and encounter us like brave men hand to hand, and we shall soon see whether these infidels can resist the slaughtering sabre of the true-believers."[196][197]

At an apt moment, the fire-fight with the enemy would cease and Janissary would charge into the enemy fighting individually with their bladed personal weapons. Typically, the Janissary would attack, "in a dense mass, with swords and other weapons – usually a single rush in a wedge formation."[198] A description of Janissary massed surges, states: "boldly advanced from all quarters in close masses."[199] The attack culminating:

189	Anthing, 1813.
190	Anthing, 1813.
191	Johnson, 1988.
192	Phillips, 1803.
193	Marsigli, 1732.
194	Valentini, 1828.
195	Alison, 1840.
196	Watts, 1997.
197	Aksan, 2002.
198	Nicolle, 1995.
199	Valentini, 1828.

"No sooner did the ... [Janissary] ... perceive that the enemy were approaching their ... [entrenchments] ... than they sallied forth with their redoubtable ... [scimitar] ... in their hands, and commenced a furious attack on the French squares."[200]

There is a 1787 Russian account, of a sword attack where it mentions, "the Turks, with their sabres and their poniards, made sad havoc among ... [the Russian Soldiers]."[201] The poniard is a small, slim dagger.

There is a direct 18th Century historical parallel with the Janissary mass Infantry attack with their Kilij: scimitar-swords, and that of the Highlands' charge. Both types of attacks were intended as battlefield shock tactics. Key differences can be seen, the tactic of Highlands' clans involved use of firearms during their actual charging attack, within the last 60 yards: 55 feet, relying on the smoke from the discharge of their weapons providing cover from view. Highlands' attack was highly dependent on speed and use of ground to give cover from the opposing troops' musket fire. Speed and momentum were so important to the Highlanders, that they preferred attacking downhill against an opponent. Highlanders, it is said, would discard their lower body clothing, prior to an attack to increase their speed and agility. Highlanders are known to have crouched low to the ground before making their final rush. Compared to the Highlands' clans, an account of the Janissary sword charge against a formed French line in Egypt, at the Battle of Heliopolis, appears to have been a direct dash:

"But ... valor could affect nothing against European steadiness and discipline; the ... [Turkish] ... were received in front by a murderous rolling fire, and charged at the same time, while disordered by their rush forward, in flank. In a few minutes they were mown down and destroyed"[202].

BATTLEFIELD HEAD-HUNTING

A 17th Century illustration depicts a Deli Cavalry Soldier holding a decapitated captive head[203]. At the 1810 Russian-Turkish Battle of Battin, it was commented, how a Russian Infantry column was destroyed entering the Turkish encampment trenches, "and the bravest of his followers who crossed it left their heads in the hands of the Turks, who fought like desperadoes."[204] Head collecting was a key aspect of Turkish military practice. In one account from the Russian-Turkish Wars,

"the Grand Vizier wrote to the ... [Sultan] ... that so numerous were the heads taken off the infidel, that they would make a bridge from earth to heaven."[205]

"It is the common custom after an action, when the Grand Vizier returns to his tent, for the Soldiers to line the path with heads which have been thus chopped off."[206]

Beheadings of the dead and wounded in battle were a common practice, and frequently occurred on a massive scale. Soldiers even carried a special weapon for the task: "Every Turk ... carries with him ... a long, and somewhat curved dagger or knife (the inward curve having the sharp edge), called a Kinschal, which he uses principally in cutting off heads."[207] At the 1811 Turkish crossing of the Danube, there was a similar account of a Russian repulse, where the Russian commander lost, "2,000 of his best troops ... [when] ... the Turks, with deafening shouts and sabre in hand, sallied out of their ... [entrenchments] ... and cut-off the heads of the slain and unfortunate wounded."[208]

A German commentator, noted somewhat disparagingly, head-hunting was mainly the actions of a bad element, "[in the Turkish] ... Army ... the rabble, who do nothing but plunder the dead and cut-off heads after a victory"[209]. That same commentator noted, in the, "field, the Grand Vizier appears

---

200	Alison, 1842.
201	Anthing, 1813.
202	Alison, 1842.
203	Ralamb, 1658.
204	Alison, 1841.
205	Alison, 1840.
206	Eton, 1798.
207	Valentini, 1828.
208	Alison, 1841.
209	Valentini, 1828.

as a man who has nothing else to do than to receive heads and ears"[210]. Modern historical accounts record the Turkish practice of battlefield head-hunting, and its financial incentive:

> "Chopping off the corpses' heads is quite appalling for the modern observer just as much as it was for the contemporaries. One might collect the heads of the enemy corpses on the battlefield ... in the hopes of material reward, as revealed in countless Ottoman narrative sources."[211]

It is known, "heads of the enemy's subjects are valued by the ... [Ottoman] ... Government at a certain price, and for every one that is brought in five sequins ... [a Venetian gold coin] ... are paid out of the treasury."[212] A passage from an Egyptian campaign account, describes the tent of the Turkish Grand Bashaw [Pasha]: Admiral and General in Egypt, in 1800:

> "[who] ... sat in state on velvet cushions distributing rewards in money to every Turk who brought a Frenchman's head, and they were scattered through the fields in search of heads and were not very nice as to how or where they obtained them; it was said that some of our ... [British] ... Soldiers' heads were among them. I went to view the horrid spectacle of a pile of heads, and beheld with detestation the exulting manner in which they brought them in and the way they kicked them about"[213].

An English diplomat's account from Egypt, also pointed to a transactional and profit motive to head collecting, by Soldiers:

> "a principle of self-interest seems to pervade all ranks; and this is carried so far, that I have seen the heads of their own companions displayed before the Grand Vizier at the Battle of Heliopolis, merely to receive the reward attached to every man who brings the head of an enemy."[214]

Recorded, in an English journal of the Egyptian campaign:

> "Some Albanians, who pushed on, got hold of five unfortunate French Soldiers, whose heads they unmercifully cut-off, and brought back with them, to claim the reward of their barbarity; for a certain sum is, given by the Turkish Commanders for the head or ears of an enemy."[215]

Napoleonic Period Turkish Soldier's pay was a daily-rate of one penny and two-pence, using the British currency of the period as an example[216]; by comparison a British Soldier receive one shilling. Janissary received only a small amount of pay, even by Turkish standards: "Infantry ... receive rather small pay."[217] The pay that was received, was only enough for them to buy, "bows, arrows and clean collars."[218] Extra money, such as bonuses – "were given for distinguished service, as when the survivors of the Serdengecti: Head-Risker, and Dil Kihc: Naked Sword ... [Soldiers] ... got extra pay"[219]. Head-hunting was therefore a lucrative business, offering financial rewards to those who could collect heads. An account of the Ottoman Governor of Acre during Napoleon's siege, during the major French assaults against his palace citadel, described how,

> "Djezzar ... [the Ottoman Governor] ... was sitting in a conspicuous place, surrounded by the mutilated members of the assailants, and by turns rewarding such as brought him heads and distributing ... [musket] ... cartridges, they were busily employed in preserving his residence and himself from destruction."[220]

The practice of paying for heads, continued up to the Sultan:

---

210   Valentini, 1828.
211   Sakul, 2012.
212   Eton, 1798.
213   Low, 1911.
214   Morier, 1801.
215   Walsh, 1803.
216   Morier, 1801.
217   Dalvimart, 1802.
218   Nicolle, 1995.
219   Nicolle, 1995.
220   Camden, 1814.

"They cut-off the heads of the dead as well as of the living, and collect them in the same manner as the heads, claws, or snouts of noxious wild beasts are delivered to the authorities appointed to reward the slayers. The custom, which has been questioned by modern historians, of collecting the noses and tips of the ears of their enemies, is literally true. When, after a successful affair, the quantity of heads becomes too considerable for conveyance, those smaller salted parts are forwarded in sacks, as testimonials of their good fortune. The … [Sultan] … awards payment for these trophies of extirpation, but prefers receiving entire heads, in order that they may be fixed on poles in the capital, with all suitable … [brilliant display]."[221]

In general, it appears that Turkish would opportunistically collect heads anytime during a battle: "All those who had been killed or wounded had their heads cut-off by the Turks and Arabs."[222] An English account from Napoleon's siege of Acre, which involved a combined British and Turkish sally-attack on the French besieging entrenchments during which they were compelled to retreat; it was complained: "the … [Turkish] … agreeably to the usual barbarity of their practice, were more active in collecting heads, than in endeavoring to annoy their opponents."[223] A similar incident is recorded during the Battle of Aboukir where General Bonaparte saw an opportunity to finally breakthrough the Turkish camp entrenchments. Said to have seen large numbers of Soldiers leave their trenches to collect prize-heads, whereupon he launched a successful counterattack finally breaking into the Turkish camp having caught the defenders completely disorganized as they were too preoccupied collecting heads[224].

European commentators saw head-hunting as, "barbarous usages of the Turks"[225]; but not militarily effective, and somewhat typical of the 18th Century mindset,

"The Prince de Ligne observed, on this practice of the Turks, to cut-off the heads of the wounded or prisoners, that it was more formidable in appearance than reality; for it could do no harm to the dead, it was often a relief to the wounded, and that it was rather an advantage to the unhurt, as it left them no chance of escape but in victory."[226][227]

Commentators in the 18th Century, were highly critical of atrocities committed by Turkish troops, such as the wanton killing and decapitation of prisoners[228]. Turkish Soldiers were also known to accept foreign Soldiers' surrender, such as that of the French Garrison of the Ionian Islands, and along the Dalmatian coast, in 1799. French prisoners of war, repatriated by 1802, were treated no differently to any other European prisoner of war in the Napoleonic Period. Instances where Turkish decapitated dead prisoners are known – the explanation, it this act was not for any financial motivation, or even as an act of barbarity, but rather as a bureaucratic action, "to prove that the captive neither ran away nor suffered an unauthorized execution during the march."[229] This act of accounting for heads, may have been common practice, as one early Napoleonic account mentions a specific number of heads being presented to the Grand Vizier, who, "had upwards of forty heads brought to him on the field of battle."[230] All these heads were paid for by the Grand Vizier himself, and he was ultimately paid by the Sultan, when these heads were bagged and sent to Constantinople as part of the reporting on the progress of the Army in the war.

221	Valentini, 1828.
222	Walsh, 1803.
223	Camden, 1814.
224	Scott, 1827.
225	Valentini, 1828.
226	Valentini, 1828.
227	Alison, 1841.
228	Eton, 1798.
229	Sakul, 2012.
230	Wittman, 1803.

CHAPTER 5: INFANTRY ORGANIZATION

The 1798 Pamphlet[231], outlined organization for the Levend Chiftlik Regiment, and its Officer's ranks. New Order Army ranks differed from Janissary adopting a new rank structure derived from French Army Regulations of the period. A New Order Army Infantry Regiment was commanded by a Bin Bachi [Bimbashi]: traditionally a Chief of One Thousand, commanding twelve Buluks: Companies composed of 1,600 Soldiers and Officers. A Regiment was divided into two Sub-Divisions of six Buluks: Companies, headed by Majors, the Aga-yi Yemen (Major of the Right), and the Aga-yi Yesar (Major of the Left). Each Buluks: Company was composed of 90 Soldiers and 10 Officers, and led by a Yuzbasi: Chief of One Hundred. Buluks: Companies were divided into nine Soldier Odas: Sub-Unit Companies[232], or French Platoons commanded by an Onbasi: Chief of Ten. The Army Commander was known as a Seraskier[233][234][235].

The 1796 General Aubert du Bayet Mission found its Infantry trainees from the Boustangees[236]. When trainees were sufficiently trained, two Infantry Regiments were raised from among other Boustangees. Topchees [Topijis]: Artillery provided a Regiment armed with hybrid designed Turkish-French light cannon. Another ten Infantry Regiments are reported to have been raised: two raised in Kutahiyeh (modern Kutahya), a city in Western Turkey, on the Porsuk River; and eight in Karamania [Carmania; Caramania], the Southern Mediterranean coast of Anatolia. These were the Anatolian Segban Provincial Militia Regiments, which may have had a modified organization, as each were comprised of ten Fusilier Buluks: Companies (100 Soldiers each), and one Artillery Buluks: Company[237]. This implies that the parent Topchees: Artillery Regiment had at least eight to ten Buluks: Companies, to meet the demand for all the new Regiments, with some 80 to 100 cannons in total – if that number was ever achieved.

▼ Levend Chiftlik Regiment Organization with 12 Buluks: Companies, and Artillery Buluks: Company (with 12 cannons: one per Infantry Buluks).

▼ Uskudar and Anatolian Regiments' Organization with 10 Buluks: Companies (five are mounted), and Artillery Buluks: Company (with 10 cannons: one per Infantry Buluks).

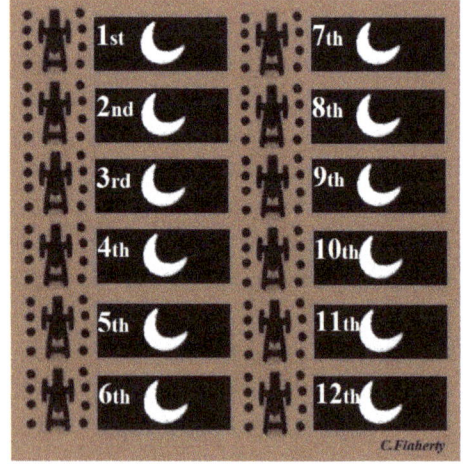
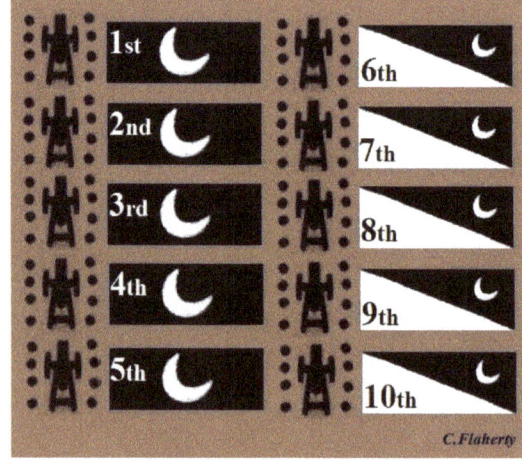

---

231   Raif, 1798.
232   Barbir, 2014.
233   Raif, 1798.
234   Shaw, 1965.
235   Johnson, 1988.
236   Roubicek, 1978.
237   Roubicek, 1978.

Between 1802 and 1806 New Order Army Regulars' Barracks were built for the new Provincial Militia at Ankara, Bolu, Kastamonu, Kutahya, Kayseri, Nigde, Kirsehir, Corum, Mentese, and Izmir[238]. It is known that Soldiers for training came:

> "from … private Armies of the leading notables of Anatolia … notables contributed men to the new Army for specific periods of two or three years, so they would get training and weapons from the central Government, and could then return home to bolster the provincial forces."[239]

Elsewhere, New Order Army Regulars were housed in buildings previously used by local Policing. Provincial Militia men came to the Uskudar Barracks for a six-month training period, in numbers approaching 5,000 a year. Prior to the New Order Army suppression in 1807[240][241], there appears to have been up to three, or four New Order Army Infantry Regiments created, that included: Boustangees (Sultan's Gardeners) Musketeer Regiment (1794); Levend Chiftlik Regiment (1799); Uskudar Regiment (1802); and, New Order Army Marines (1804). Other Regiments (in effect Orta: Battalions) that might have come into existence, were some of the Sultan's Household Infantry, and at least eight to ten Anatolian Segban Provincial Militia Regiments. In addition, there were Arnaut: Albanian Infantry, whose military ethos, and training had a strong connection with typical European Armies' style of warfighting.

NUMERICALLY WEAK ARMY COMPOSITION

In the late-18th Century, the Turkish Army was reputed to be large, "[the] … collected force of the Empire is said to amount to 400,000 men."[242] A survey of the Ottoman Empire's actual military strength only counted some 186,400 effective Soldiers[243]. Vast numbers of Janissary institutionally represented a social welfare system: "a muster roll of close to half a million … paid a fee each … [with only] … probably 1 in 10 were actual fighting forces."[244] It is known, that by 1761, Standing Army Regulars registered for use in campaign was 55,731 which had been progressively falling since the start of the 18th Century[245]. It has been stated, that by the late-18th Century, the: "Ottoman Empire was only capable of raising 30,000 troops for a major campaign."[246] These troops represented, "Janissary, Artillerists, and Gun-Carriage Drivers"[247]. The Turkish Army at the Battle of Forhani, in 1789 illustrates a numerically weak Army composition, out of a force of 40,000 it is known that the two Cavalry wings were around 20,000 and 15,000 respectively leaving only about 5,000 at the most as Infantry to defend the major entrenched camp. The significance of these numbers, is that the battle is usually represented as being disproportionally in favor of the Turkish Army, having greater numbers as there were 40,000 against 18,000 Austrians and 7,000 Russians[248]. Illustrative of how weak Turkish forces were, at the opening maneuvers pre-empting the battle it is mentioned Austrians and Russians only encountered some 4,000 Sipahi: Cavalry, and 2,000 Infantry, with two cannons[249]. Similar small numbers can be seen at the Battle of El-Hanka [Belbeis], on 16 May 1801, which was a victory of the Grand Vizier over the French. At that battle, the Grand Vizier had an assembled force of about 15,000 Soldiers[250]. This force included Tahir Pasha, with a chosen corps of 3,000 Cavalry[251].

238   Shaw, 1965.
239   Shaw, 1965.
240   Shaw, 1965.
241   Uyar, 2009.
242   McLean, 1818.
243   Eton, 1798.
244   Aksan, 2002.
245   Agoston, 2011.
246   Nicolle, 1998.
247   Agoston, 2011
248   Anthing, 1813.
249   Anthing, 1813.
250   Walsh, 1803.
251   Walsh, 1803.

The only other troops at the Grand Vizier's disposal were 500 of Djezzar Pasha troops, "well-armed and appointed"[252]. Later British account-returns, during the Egyptian campaign gives typical Turkish Division sizes and troops available: "This evening 500 Turks joined the Army ... [5, to 6,000] ... more were hourly expected with the ... [Captain-Pasha]."[253] There is also a later mention of similarly small, numbered Turkish Divisions being available during British operations in Egypt, "500 Turks remained in the rear during the whole action"; or a detached column under, "Colonel Spencer ... with 4,000 Turkish troops"[254]. Several other mentions of Turkish troops during the Egyptian campaign tend to suggest small numbers of actual Soldiers available, such as:

Albanians, with Colonel Stewart's Column:	1,000
Turkish Regulars under the Captain-Pasha*:	1,100
Irregulars under the Captain-Pasha:	1,500
Turkish Cavalry under the Captain-Pasha:	600
Total	4,200

*The Captain-Pasha was the Supreme Commander of the Turkish Navy[255][256].

By the time of the British and allied investment of Cairo and Giza, the Turkish Army under the Grand Vizier, was similarly small, as it amounted to about 12,000 Cavalry and 7,000 Infantry"[257]. This later account tends to suggest that Turkish Armies were typically smaller than those seen in Europe in the same period. In effect, corresponding to typical divisional tactical units of the Napoleonic Period Corps, that usually consisted of as many as 10,000 Infantry, or some 4,000 Cavalry.

The Turkish Army in Egypt appear to have mainly formed small contingents on campaign. For instance, a force of 8,000 Janissary, arrived with the convoy of Sir Sydney Smith, in Egypt[258]. The Janissary forces' actual combat strength may have been even weaker, as it appears within this force, there was a, "leading Division of 4,000 men ... with five pieces of cannon"[259]; and the 1,000 Soldiers in the Levend Chiftlik Regiment. The rest of these were likely to have been trades persons, camp followers and attendants. Turkish troops that arrived with the Grand Vizier's Army, in Egypt was said to have been some 80,000 Soldiers[260][261]. In terms of actual combat strength, the Infantry component in Egypt appears undersized compared to the overall number in the Army. Actual troop numbers drop radically, as the two main Infantry forces were 7,000 Arnaut: Albanian troops organized into three Regiments[262][263]. The remaining force, possibly some 13,000 Janissary appear to have been organized into four major Contingents, raised in Europe, or "raised in Syria for the Garrisons of Aleppo, Damascus, and Cairo"[264]; who were likely Imperial Janissary Regiments. The rest of the Grand Vizier's Army, in Egypt were its Cavalry, which were known to be a large force that consisted of 25,000 Soldiers[265][266]. There was also a small light Artillery Column of 19 six-pounder cannons, and five-inch howitzers[267]. Later in the campaign in Egypt, much smaller forces are recorded, the largest of which

252 Walsh, 1803
253 Walsh, 1803.
254 Walsh, 1803.
255 Dalvimart, 1802.
256 McLean, 1818.
257 Wittman, 1803.
258 Alison, 1842.
259 Alison, 1842.
260 Morier, 1801.
261 Alison, 1842.
262 Low, 1911.
263 Morier, 1801.
264 Morier, 1801.
265 Morier, 1801.
266 Alison, 1842.
267 Morier, 1801.

appears to have been a 6,000 force of Janissary in the village of Matarieh [Matharieh], at the battle of Heliopolis, in 1800[268]. An English journal account from the later Egyptian campaign tends to confirm the relative low number of actual Turkish troops available:

> "In September 1800, the Grand Vizier supposed himself to be at the head of 35,000 Soldiers. Brigadier General ... [George Koehler, a British Artillery Officer] ... presumed to think his highness deceived in his computation, and ventured to declare his opinion, that the troops did not exceed 7 or 8,000."[269]

Weak overall Army numbers could be related to Janissary Orta: Battalions in the 18th Century operating in practice, in a much different way from European or New Order Army Infantry Regiments. For this reason, the description, "Chambers"[270], is used to correctly describe an Orta: Battalion. At the end of the 18th Century, the size of Orta: Battalion's organization varied significantly: "The number ... composing each ... varies, and is not limited; for, in general ... [one] ... which has gained the greatest renown in war exploits is sought after by those who wish to enlist."[271] The size of the Orta: Battalion organization had reached unmanageable proportions:

> "The number of ... [Janissary] ... in each... [Orta: Battalion] ... is not fixed, but depends upon its celebrity; from a vanity natural enough, greater numbers enrolling themselves in such ... as are most distinguished; the number in some is extremely great, that of the ... [35th Cemaat] ... amounting to nearly thirty thousand."[272]

It should be noted, by this time a new category of Janissary had emerged: namely the 'Economic Janissary'; not Soldiers but massive numbers of tradespersons joining Orta: Battalions to secure business activities[273]. By the 18th Century, entry into the Janissary had opened to enrolled men who, "[practiced] ... the lowest trades ... [and had] ... nothing military but the name Janissary"[274]. Economic Janissary would display their Orta badge over business premises[275]. It is known, "selling Janissary certificates that enabled their holders to draw pay and receive daily food rations ... became a lucrative business for Officers and bureaucrats."[276]

A 1798 survey of the actual strength of the Turkish Army, recorded some 113,400 militarily active Janissary[277]. Distributing this total number among the 101 traditional Orta: Battalions would have given each of these up to 1,200 or so Janissary Soldiers. Only a select number of Janissary were ready for combat at any time, and came from further afield than Constantinople. Such as Janissary sent to major City Garrison, who were then double-enrolled in the local Imperial Janissary Regiments, which were part of the Province Governors' Armies:

> "When the Grand Vizier assembles an Army, the different ... [Pasha] ... choose out such of the ... [Janissary] ... in their respective provinces as are fittest for the campaign, register their names, order them an allowance for their journey, and send them to join the Army"[278].

There is also a reference, from around the 1740s where a Janissary could be censured for bad behavior and one of the punishments was being marked-out for, "dangerous assignments on campaign."[279] An English journal from the Egyptian campaign mentions a corps of Turks, under Ibrahim Pasha

---

268 Alison, 1842.
269 Walsh, 1803.
270 Morier, 1801.
271 Morier, 1801.
272 McLean, 1818.
273 Sunar, 2006.
274 Eton, 1798.
275 Sunar, 2006,
276 Agoston, 2011
277 Eton, 1798.
278 McLean, 1818.
279 Barbir, 2014.

of Aleppo that had 2,000 Soldiers[280]. There is also a 1799 account from an English traveler who calculated that the full Garrison in Aleppo, there were only 15,000 Janissary, and while had, "superior valor … [they were] … little acquainted with the use of arms or aspect of battle."[281] An earlier account from 1708, reviewing the state of the Damascus Janissary, "found … of 1,231 members of the corps, the majority were unfit for service because they were either too old and feeble or underage"[282]. Following this review, "numbers were reduced to 913 (of whom 35 were pensioners) … distributed through eight Cavalry units (Cemaat) and forty-two Companies (Boluk) of Foot Soldiers."[283] The military effectiveness of the two corps of Janissary in Damascus was likely open to question, as it is known by 1806, the City Garrison, and Imperial Janissary constantly feuded, and this had been the case for decades[284]. It appears that actual military service, apart from protecting the pilgrimage route, by the mid-18th Century was rarely experienced[285][286]. It is also known that some of the Janissary from the Damascus Garrison may have ended up in French service, as a unit of Syrian Janissary Infantry, formed in 1799.

LEVEND ORTA: BATTALIONS

Throughout the 18th Century, Provincial Levend [Leventi] formed an Armed Militia, or Armed Mercenaries[287]. Turkish peasants were paid under short-duration contracts as Foot Musketeer Soldiers. Typically, Levend, "were recruited for an initial period of six months, with ensuing two-month renewals of the contract"[288]. Use of the Levend, it was said, was abolished around 1775. Soldiers called Levend nevertheless continued to exist well after that date, including naming one of the first New Order Army Regiments – the Levend Chiftlik Regiment. The Levend constituted the bulk of the Turkish Infantry, and many units were directly recruited by the Central Government, being referred to as Miri: State Levend. The Levend were also the basis of the Armed Retinue of a Regional Commander and were called Kapili: Household Levend. Traditional Levend Militia Officer rank system had a simple organization[289]:

Bolukbasi	Buluks: Company Captain
Bayrakdar [Bairaktar]	Standard Bearer
Cavus	Sergeant or Disciplinary Officer
Odabasi	Barrack Room Chief (Janissary Title)

It is known, Levend Militia were organized into Companies. Each Buluks: Company was commanded by a Bolukbasi: Captain, and there was a Basbolukbasi: Head-Captain in command overall[290]. From the second half of the 1730s, Levend Officer ranks such as the Bolukbasi changed, "the commander of a 100 … [Soldier] … unit being called a Yuzbasi, a 500 … unit, Besyuzbasi and a 1000 … unit … [a Bimbashi]."[291] The newer 1730s rank of Yuzbasi [Ynz-Bachi; Youzbashee]: Captain, and Bimbashi: Major, were later incorporated into the New Order Army rank system based on European military organization. Likewise, ranks such as the Cavus: Sergeant, were incorporated into the New Order Army rank system as a conventional Non-Commissioned Officer: Sergeant. Made senior to the Odabasi: New Order Army Non-Commissioned Officer: Corporal.

280 Walsh, 1803.
281 Browne, 1799.
282 Barbir, 2014.
283 Barbir, 2014.
284 Grehan, 2007.
285 Douwes, 2000.
286 Barbir, 2014.
287 Buyukakca, 2007.
288 Buyukakca, 2007.
289 Buyukakca, 2007.
290 Buyukakca, 2007.
291 Buyukakca, 2007.

The Levend organization included Odas: Sub-Unit Companies[292]. The early-18th Century recruitment of paid State Mercenaries: Miri Levends, were used in the Standing Army as Dragoons, or Infantry Companies of 50 to 100 Soldiers each, commanded by an Ayan: Provincial Notables, or Gentry[293][294]. Ayan were local notables with administrative control, primarily tax collectors, these could also be heads of Janissary Garrisons.

Contracted Mercenary Battalions in different ethnic regions of the Ottoman Empire were identified as Fusilier Tufenkcis: Fusiliers[295]. It is known, that the Provincial Militaria Musketeers had their own internal organization, dress, and separate Barracks.

1794 BOUSTANGEES (SULTAN'S GARDENERS) MUSKETEER REGIMENT

Forming a separate Orta: Battalion from the ordinary Janissary, the Boustangees were the Guards of the palace gardens, and the Sultan when he goes into the field[296]. Responsible for the maintenance, policing and defence of some 70 Imperial Estates as well as the coasts around Constantinople. The Boustangees Musketeer Regiment [Bostanci Tufenkjisi; Bostandji Musketeers] can be related to the founding of the New Order Army:

> "The first hundred … [New Order Army] … Infantry were recruited from … Constantinople's … poor, with Officers and drill masters drawn from Russian or German renegades. This Regiment of 1794 was also camouflaged in the hope of making it acceptable to the traditionalists by being attached to the old Bostanci-i Hass … [Bostaniyan-i Hassa] … Elite Infantry Guard, and called the Bostanci Tufenkjisi … or Bostanci Musketeers."[297][298]

The title: Tufenkjisi [Tufenkcis]: Musketeers was commonly used for Levend [Leventi], or Segban Foot Musketeer Orta: Battalions[299]. It is also explained about the Boustangee Musketeer Regiment's origin:

> "The literal meaning of the word … [Boustangees] … is Gardeners, is not sufficiently indicative of the employments of those who bear it, which are of a very diversified nature … they compose the first, or outer guard of the Seraglio, and a detachment, selected from them and called Assequis, forms a part of the Sultan's Bodyguard, whom they always accompany, armed with sabres, which they wear slung over their shoulders, and carrying white staves, to indicate that they are the executors of his commands."[300]

It is known, Boustangees were a large Orta: Battalion, with many enrollees: "Their number amounts to several thousands, and out of them is formed the Bodyguard of the Sultan."[301][302] A modern account gives their number as, "only a few thousand"[303]. A 1798 survey of the actual strength of the Turkish Army, records that the number of Boustangees was 12,000 Soldiers[304]. Modern accounts say that the Boustangees, "were almost as resistant to change as the … [Janissary]."[305][306] Nevertheless, it was stated:

---

292 Barbir, 2014.
293 Buyukakca, 2007.
294 Sakul, 2014.
295 Barbir, 2014.
296 Eton, 1798.
297 Shaw, 1965.
298 Nicolle, 1998.
299 Buyukakca, 2007.
300 McLean, 1818.
301 Dalvimart, 1802.
302 McLean, 1818.
303 Nicolle, 1998.
304 Eton, 1798.
305 Shaw, 1965.
306 Nicolle, 1998.

"In the year 1796, the Turkish military force was improved, by a levy of twelve thousand men, who were armed and instructed in a manual exercise and field movements, on the principles of those adopted in Great Britain … it was resolved they should belong nominally to the … [Boustangees]"[307].

1799 LEVEND CHIFTLIK REGIMENT

The Levend Chiftlik [Chifflick; Levend Tchiftlik; Shifflick (modern mistake)] Regiment was formed around 1792, trained under Omar Aga Corps, and instruction from Lieutenant-General Menant, Lieutenants Ranchoup and Luzin, along with six Sergeants sent by the French Ministry of War[308]. 1798, is known as a key date, as a Pamphlet in French outlining the reforms was published. The Pamphlet outlined reforms taken to create the, "Pour le Corps discipline a l'Europeenne, de Levend Tchiftlik": European Discipline Corps from Levend Tchiftlik[309]. Historical accounts from the 1799 Siege of Acre identify the Levend Chiftlik Regiment as disembarking from HMS Tigre (8 May 1799), and playing a crucial part in the battle[310]. Actual spelling of Chiftlik is subject to some variations, as it is commonly spelled "Chifflick"[311]. There has also been a modern misspelling: Shifflick Regiment in various web forums, the confusion caused by a wargaming publication that mistakenly use information gleaned from older-period illustration used for painting wargaming figures; namely, a French 19th Century color card illustrating cut-out toy soldiers: titled "Turkish Soldiers"[312]. The name: Chiftlik, has a specific significance, as it is the phonic pronunciation for Ciftlik: Ottoman landholding system creating hereditary farms worked by peasants. It is known that these aristocratic estates were owned by Ottoman nobility, and the Sultan. The Regimental name - Levend Chiftlik, was in fact more a unit nickname, relating directly to the Soldiers' connection with the Sultan's Estate where the main training Barracks had been built by 1798[313].

1802 USKUDAR REGIMENT

It is generally accepted that the second New Order Army Regiment was established at Uskudar in 1799[314]. A modern version of a Uskudar Soldier is identified as an: "Neferi of the Nizam-i Cedit 2nd Orta 'Provincial Militaria' circa 1795"[315]. This odd attribution may refer to one of the several Anatolian Segban Provincial Militia Regiments that were formed; however, it is not entirely clear how an Orta: Battalion number was assigned, or if these were used, as these Regiments more likely had territorial titles. Provincial Militia Reserves recruits sent to Uskudar Barracks, were drawn from the following Anatolian districts, where they returned to serve, or collected into the 1806 Regulars' Army of Kadi Abdurrahman Pasha:

Aksehir Segban Provincial Militia Regiment
Ankara Segban Provincial Militia Regiment
Aydin Segban Provincial Militia Regiment
Beygehir Segban Provincial Militia Regiment
Bolu and Viransehir Segban Provincial Militia Regiment
Kastamonu Segban Provincial Militia Regiment
Kayseri Segban Provincial Militia Regiment
Kutahya Segban Provincial Militia Regiment
Nigde Segban Provincial Militia Regiment

307   McLean, 1818.
308   Shaw, 1965.
309   Raif, 1798.
310   Mostert, 2008.
311   Clarke, 1816.
312   Kernan, 2011.
313   Raif, 1798.
314   Uyar, 2009.
315   Nicolle, 1998.

Known as the second of the New Order Army Regiments, the Uskudar, are described as, "[a] … Provincial Militaria of Mounted Infantry"[316]. It was the case, only half the Regiment was trained as, "Cavalry so they could return to form the local Militias of the Provincial Governors and district notables."[317] The Turkish often trained Foot Soldiers to fight mounted. In the 17th Century, the 64th and 65th Cemaat Janissary Cavalry Orta: Battalion had existed. Long after disbandment, in 1623, there is a 1789 account that illustrates how Janissary were used as mounted Infantry: "[Janissary] … having mounted behind the … [Sipahi: Cavalry] … leaped down, and fought by the side of their horse … [after the battle] … re-mounted their horses, took to flight."[318] European accounts from the 18th Century comment how the Turkish Soldier was trained as both a Foot-Soldier, and Dragoon, "according to circumstances. If the … [Sipahi: Cavalry] … loses his horse, he immediately takes his place among the Infantry; and, in the same manner, the Janissary will mount, without hesitation, the first horse which chance throws in his way."[319] Mounted Uskudar Soldiers likely used the same type of saddles as the rest of the Sipahi: Cavalry, which was a high backed saddle-seat, incorporating a small square saddle blanket, which could be a variety of color combinations. The major difference was its stirrup arrangement:

> "The Turkish saddle is somewhat inconvenient to Europeans; and as spurs are not employed, the rider is obliged to have recourse to his stirrups when he wishes the animal on which he is mounted to quicken his pace."[320]

SULTAN'S HOUSEHOLD INFANTRY

Prior to 1826, the Sultan's Household retained several Orta: Battalions of Solak [Solacchi]: Bodyguard Archers, Peik [Peyks]: Bodyguard Axemen, and Boustangees, who formed one of several Foot Guard units in the palace[321]. By the late-18th Century, various armed Household Guard units had probably amalgamated into a musket armed Battalion. Such an amalgamation may have been practical, as the Turkish by this time tended to rely on 1,000 Soldier Orta: Battalion as the main functional Musketeer unit on campaign. It has been suggested, Solak, "were … [only a small] … Ceremonial Guard for the Sultan's palace."[322] The Grand Vizier, as the Army Commander was provided with a Personal Guard, along with the other Janissary retained by him[323]. An 1803 account noted Solak as part of the Personal Guard of the Grand Vizier, identified by their uniforms, who: "wore yellow dresses, decorated with ribbons of different colors hanging from the shoulders, and brass helmets on their heads."[324]

An 1850 illustration-lithograph, shows a figure, called: "Choubara Neferi, Soldat of the 1st Reform of Sultan Mahmud II."[325] The figure wears a yellow Cahouk: quilted top hat, with a collarless yellow jersey-jacket, with dark blue-grey Russian pants, and low black Turkish riding boots completing the dress. The 1850 depiction is near identical to a 1907 illustration describing uniforms under, "Regne du Sultan Abdul … [Mahmud II] … Avan l'Introduction de l'Uniforme Europeenn": before the introduction of the European uniform, called a Soldat d'Infanterie: Infantry Soldier[326]. Depicted wearing a yellow low collared jersey-jacket, with salmon-pink Russian pants, and red Turkish slipper-shoes, with a yellow Cahouk. The yellow uniform, and headgear suggests either a Solak, or Peik Guardsman trained and uniformed as a New Order Army Soldier. Solak and Peik Guardsman

---

316	Nicolle, 1998.
317	Shaw, 1965.
318	Wright, 1799.
319	Valentini, 1828.
320	Wittman, 1803.
321	Tyrrell, 1910.
322	Nicolle, 1998.
323	Johnson, 1988.
324	Wittman, 1803.
325	Brindesi, 1850.
326	Sevket, 1907.

merging, as part of a newly trained unit, may explain the apparent confusion, as earlier references tend to reverse the titles[327]. A post-1826 Soldier wearing a yellow jersey-jacket, with yellow Fez tassel is known, as is an 1861 2nd Guard Regiment wearing yellow jacket facings and a yellow Fez tassel. It is suspected, in the later years of Sultan Selim III, a yellow uniformed Palace unit was formed, and continued to wear New Order Army uniforms during the early-years under Sultan Mahmud II.

SEGBAN FOOT MUSKETEER ORTA: BATTALIONS

The Segban [Sekhan; Sekban]: Hound Keepers, had been a Palace Guard unit under Sultan Mehmed II, and later incorporated into the Janissary as a third cohort of Orta: Battalions numbered 1st to 34th [328]. By 1596, their number had risen to 20,000 Soldiers. After this date Segban Soldiers were employed as Garrison Guards. Segban also refers to the formation of Mercenary Musketeers from the 17th Century onwards[329]. By the 18th Century, Segban had become a Rural Militia[330]. Associated with Turkish-Anatolia, where local peasants were organized into Musketeer Orta: Battalions, and operated as paid Mercenaries, "attached to the households of Provincial Governors and other high officials."[331] Segban Foot Musketeer Orta: Battalions, composed of Provincial Levies in Vilayet: Governor's Provinces, provided the majority of the Standing Army's Infantry on campaign. Hired for the duration of a campaign, or as part of the long-term security force for a local Province, these Auxiliary Troops were trained and led by Janissary Officers. In practical terms, Segban Foot Musketeer Orta: Battalions were commonly filled with Levend[332]. Under the early military reforms of Sultan Selim III the Segban were identified as a Provincial Militia Reserves, that by 1801 were rolled into an expansion program where, "half were trained as Infantry to be added to the Levend Chiftlik Regiment, and half as Cavalry, to return to their provincial bases in support of the local Governor."[333] From around 1801, some 12,000 Segban Provincial Militia Reserves recruits were sent to Uskudar Barracks drawn from the following Anatolian districts:

Aksehir	1,000	Kastamonu	1,000
Ankara	2,000	Kayseri	1,000
Aydin	1,000	Kutahya	1,000
Beygehir	2,000	Nigde	1,000
Bolu and Viransehir	2,000		

1808 SEGBAN-I CEDID: NEW SEGBAN ARMY

A group of, "new Regiments of Mustafa Bayraktar Pasha ... [were] ... organized at the same time as those of Selim III, ... called ... [the] ... Sekhan-i Cedid"[334]; or Segban-i Cedid[335]. The New Segban Army, from 1807 till 1808, was formed:

> "To avoid resistance from the Janissary the new force was not called Nizam-i Cedid: New Order Army, but rather was made part of the old order, attached to the Kapikulu Ocaklari: Standing Army, after the extinct Segban: Keepers of the Hounds Corps, an affiliate of the Janissary, becoming the Segban-i Cedid: New Segban."[336]

---

327   Sevket, 1907.
328   Uyar, 2009.
329   Lapidus, 2002.
330   Nicolle, 1998.
331   Barbir, 2014.
332   Buyukakca, 2007.
333   Aksan, 2007.
334   Zurcher, 1999.
335   Shaw, 1977.
336   Shaw, 1977.

The New Segban Army consisted of 3,000 Soldiers in a, "rapid-fire rifle force", under Kadi Abdurrahman Pasha, that apparently only existed for a short period of time, till 1808[337][338]. It is possible that some post-1810 figures depicted in a set of 1907 illustration, described as, "Regne du Sultan Abdul … [Mahmud II] … Avan l'Introduction de l'Uniforme Europeenn": before the introduction of the European uniform[339], are some of these New Segban Army Soldiers, still employed; as well as some later-era uniforms from around 1818, said to show "European Model Soldiers"[340].

It is not entirely clear what type of Soldier constituted a 'rapid-fire rifle force', in the context of military technology in 1808, and it is not known if these troops were exclusively armed with rifled muskets or not. It should also be noted, more recent historical accounts, identify the Kadi Abdurrahman Pasha Corps, composed of 3,000 Musketeers from among the disbanded New Order Army Regulars[341]. Bayraktar Mustafa attempted to restore the New Order Army around the Kadi Abdurrahman Pasha Corps, adding survivors from the 1807 fighting and suppression, and other Soldiers belonging to Anatolian nobles: Karaosmanoglu and Capanoglu [Cabbaroglus] family dynasties. The New Segban Army reoccupied the Levend Chiftlik and Uskudar Barracks. By 3 October 1808 some 5,000 volunteers were enrolled[342]. Suleyman Aga, and Kadi Abdurrahman Pasha served as the military commanders. The 1808 military reformers envisaged a force of some 160,000 Soldiers divided into 100 Boluk: Regiments, organized into three Divisions. However, only 10,000 Soldiers and Officers appear to have been raised. More recent discussions on the New Segban Army, suggests it amounted to nine Anatolian Regiments – which appears to be close to the original Segban Provincial Militia Reserves that were organized throughout Anatolia, and returned to the Governors there.

POST-1809 WARTIME AD-HOC JANISSARY ORTA: BATTALIONS

Ottoman Government authorities are known to have created ad-hoc Janissary Wartime Regiments, or Orta: Battalions on a regular basis. All active Janissary in Constantinople were expected to report for service. During the Russian-Turkish War (1806 till 1812), after the disbandment of the New Order Army, there is mention of organizing new Janissary Regiments[343]. These new Regiments appear to have been composite units composed of volunteers from various Orta: Battalions and allotted to the wartime units. Some of these may have been solely composed of Janissary from the same Orta; and many were likely mixed units. Mention is made of five Janissary Regiments, being lost, taken as prisoners by the Russians, in the summer of 1811[344]. In April 1812, there is mention of three Janissary Regiments from Constantinople, consisting of 3,000 Soldiers, ordered to join the Field Army[345]. Units such as these suggest standard formations of Foot Musketeers organized into Orta: Battalion, typically numbering about 1,000 Soldiers. Modern historians give greater numbers, for a Orta: Battalion operating, by the time of Sultan Selim III, "a tactical unit numbering about 2,000 to 3,000 troops."[346] An earlier account from Egypt in 1800, indicates much smaller standard units of about 1,000 Soldiers each: "two Regiments of 200 … each deserted for no other reason, than that the Grand Vizier refused to pay them as if they had their full complement of 1,000 Soldiers."[347] The standard field commander for an Orta: Battalion was a Bimbashi: Leader of a Thousand.

---

337 Shaw, 1977.
338 Nicolle, 1998.
339 Sevket, 1907.
340 McLean, 1818.
341 Aksan, 2007.
342 Shaw, 1977.
343 Sunar, 2006.
344 Sunar, 2006.
345 Sunar, 2006.
346 Johnson, 1988.
347 Walsh, 1803.

CHAPTER 6: INFANTRY SOLDIER'S WEAPONS AND EQUIPMENT

Janissary only saw weapons when training, or preparing for a battle; other than that, they marched unarmed, transporting all their firearms by Arabaci: Transport Corps' wagons. Historically, Janissary had been axe, sword, spear, or bow armed. By the 18th Century, in addition to muskets individual Janissary carried a variety of personal weapons, such as the classic Kilij: the curve-bladed scimitar-sword. Long blade weapon scabbards were hung on two straps from the belt, or on a longer shoulder cord. Janissary commonly carried pistols, knives and steel war axes - all positioned in their cloth waist bands. Janissary carried ball bags, powder horns, and cartridge-charge bottles on bandolier, and generally had the appearance by the late-18th Century of woods persons, or hunters rather than typical-looking Soldiers, carrying their military equipment load-kit.

TURKISH MUSKETS

Typically, after 1558, it is known Janissary were increasingly free to buy their own muskets from imported gun makers. It is said,

> "[Turkish] … musket-barrels are much esteemed; but they are too heavy … They are … made round a rod of iron they twist soft old iron wire, and forge it; then they bore out the rod, part of which often remains, according as the wire was thick or thin, and the bore large or small."[348]
> Traditionally, "[Turkish] … muskets shot larger balls, had a longer range with more penetrating power compared to other European muskets"[349]. It was known, "Turkish sniper-fire … [was] … said to be more accurate than European ones … from over 500 feet range made rampart sentry walk untenable."[350]

The typical Tufenk: matchlock was known to be longer barreled, and fired a heavier ball[351]. During the earlier Long War (in the 1600s), and still likely the case in the early-18th Century, Janissary firearms fired bullets of 12 to15 grams, which approximately represented gun calibres of 13 to 14 millimeters. These muskets were 115 to 140 centimeters long, and weighed 3- to 4.5-kilograms each[352]. It is known, that even in the 18th Century, "most … [Janissary] … Tufenk (muskets) were matchlocks rather than the newer flintlocks."[353] In the 18th Century, Turkish also used a flintlock musket: Muskat Tufenkleri with a strong European influence in its design[354]. These muskets were also distinctive, a description of these weapons used by the Albanian troops in Egypt:

> "Their firearms are in general beautifully ornamented in silver and gold; their muskets are light, and are made like a tomahawk at the but-end, I imagine to be used in self-defence in cases of necessity."[355]

TURKISH RIFLED MUSKETS

Rifled musket-types are known to have been used by Janissary[356]. The rifled musket had an early introduction to the Janissary and Mameluke of Egypt, originating from the Balkan region, these typically had seven grooved barrels[357]. In Egypt, in 1800, it was noted by a British observer that the Janissary,

---

348	Eton, 1798.
349	Sakul, 2013.
350	Gush, 1975.
351	Nicolle, 1995.
352	Agoston, 2005.
353	Nicolle, 1998.
354	Nicolle, 1995.
355	Morier, 1801.
356	Nicolle, 1995.
357	Elgood, 1995.

"carry a short rifle-barrel musket, flung across the shoulder, without a bayonet. The fire of these muskets, the greater part of which are manufactured at Damascus, cannot be very brisk, as they require a considerable time to load."[358]

NEW ORDER ARMY MUSKETS AND RIFLES

Muskets used by the New Order Army were mostly imported, as Ottoman State arms factories had become notorious for badly produced guns[359]. What is known about the New Order Army muskets, these were made at a new rifle factory specifically built at the Levend Chiftlik Barracks[360]. It is said, the guns were, "superior weapons"[361]. It appears, muskets were manufactured from imported European barrels and firelocks based on the 1777 Charleville musket commonly use throughout Europe at the time. Completed weapons were also assembled in private workshops in Constantinople, being fitted with wooden stocks and smaller metal fittings copied from European models as required in Government contracts[362]. Regarding muskets being rifled, or some of these being rifled, there is an account that under Sultan Selim III, the use of rifles had begun around 1793, and that: "new-style rifles were imported in increasing quantities from France, England and Sweden."[363][364] It should be noted, in the case of France, the first rifled musket was introduced in 1793, namely the Mle 1793.

CARTRIDGE BOX AND AMMUNITION POUCHES

An 1802 illustration shows the New Order Army cartridge box[365][366]. Appearing as a more Turkish inspired design rather than the common French pattern of the period. The standard French Infantry ammunition pouch had a full covering front-flap. Containing a single wood block with holes for paper cartridges. The Turkish version appears to show two compartments, likely containing a separate wood block in each compartment, with a rounded base (the function of which is not explained). An 1806 account records, "[Turkish] … Infantry … carry … [their own cartridges, which they have made] … in a square box, in which is a small jar of oil for cleaning the gun"[367]. This might suggest that only one of the compartments had a wooden block, the other compartment used for the Soldier's cleaning supplies. The front-flap on the Turkish version only partly covers the face of the pouch.

A large ammunition pouch-box is depicted slung on its cross-strap seen in a picture of Artillery Drivers[368]. Use of ammunition pouches in the Napoleonic Period while typically associated with the New Order Army Regulars may have had a wider use in the Janissary Infantry. Several illustrations show Turkish troops with cross-belts: the figures seen from the front only[369]. An 1803 dated illustration shows a small ammunition box hanging at the back of several Turkish Soldiers, directly under the waist sash[370].

NEW ORDER ARMY BELTS AND FROGS

The likely scabbard for the 1777 Charleville musket bayonet, was either of French origin, or a Turkish copy, on a loop frog slung from either the ammunition pouch belt, or the waist belt[371]. An illus-

---

358   Wittman, 1803.
359   Yesil, 2009.
360   Shaw, 1965.
361   Shaw, 1965.
362   Yesil, 2009.
363   Shaw, 1965.
364   Roy, 2011.
365   Dalvimart, 1802.
366   Roubicek, 1978.
367   Poqueville, 1806.
368   Unknown, 1788.
369   Hochenleitter, 1788.
370   Wittman, 1803.
371   Raif, 1798.

tration of the waist belt and buckle used by a New Order Army Soldier, shows this was plain white with a brass square open frame[372][373].

NEW ORDER ARMY BAYONETS

The standard 1777 Charleville was a state-of-the-art weapon by the standards of the 18th Century, as it was one of the first socket bayonets incorporating a captive locking ring, which rotated to secure the socket to the musket sight-stud. Incorporating a simple long triangular blade, its length ranged from around 14 to 15-inches. While Charleville bayonets are depicted arming New Order Army Soldiers[374], another type is seen in original illustrations[375][376], and shows a very different configuration from standard 18th Century bayonets. The right-angle bar is longer, connecting to a sub-socket-tube. The blade appears to be a broad leaf, resembling a spear, and much shorter, possibly even being a converted spearhead. It should also be noted, an identical bayonet is depicted with a 1770 Polish Janissary[377]. A series of cartoon figures from 1798, showing 'military evolutions' (musket drill) of the New Order Army Soldiers also shows this distinctive short leaf-blade bayonet[378].

ADDITIONAL LOAD-BEARING EQUIPMENT

In Egypt, in 1800, it was noted by a British observer that the Janissary: "On a march they carry their water either in a tin canteen, or in a leathern bottle."[379] Missing from the historical record is what other types of basic Infantry equipment was adopted from European models, such as backpacks, and given to the New Order Army. Turkish Foot Soldiers, in the Napoleonic Period are known to have used load-bearing equipment. For instance, when the Arnaut Troops arrived in Egypt, three of their Regiments received British arms and accoutrements[380]. Known illustrations of the New Order Army only show Soldiers with the belt strap over the left shoulder supporting the cartridge box, and the waist belt, which had the bayonet frog presumably (as this detail is not shown usually) looped onto it. It is interesting to note, that some 50 years later, Crimean War descriptions of Turkish Infantry basic Soldiers' equipment as mostly consisting of Napoleonic Period patterns[381]. In the Crimean War, the Turkish backpack was described as large dark-colored black oil skin, and square shaped; it was based on European military designs, it contained a wooden frame. It had three straps on top to attach the blanket roll. There was a center extended strap to hold down the front flap, and to attach a large tin Russian water bottle. Soldiers were also seen using a simply made flapped sack of canvas or haversack, with a blanket tied around it. Another Crimean War account describes a roll of blanket, or a sleeping rug, slung across the back on white belts. The 'roll' could also be a carpet, which was carried by individual Soldiers to lay on the ground[382].

KILIJ: THE CURVE-BLADED SCIMITAR-SWORD

Often called, "Damascus scimitar"[383], these weapons after 1750 were rarely made from patterned-forged wootz steel, which had made these sword blades famous for their tough, shatter resistant and extremely sharp edges. It is interesting to note, that illustrations show the swords slung in their scab-

---

372	Dalvimart, 1802.
373	McLean, 1818.
374	Sevket, 1907.
375	Dalvimart, 1802.
376	Roubicek, 1978.
377	Le Prince, 1770.
378	Raif, 1798.
379	Wittman, 1803.
380	Low, 1911.
381	Norman, 1985.
382	Radcliffe, 1858.
383	Alison, 1840.

bards with the blade uppermost[384], a technique used to preserve the blade edge from wear to keep its sharpness. By the late-18th Century, Kilij: scimitar-sword were shortened. Kilij had a typical overall length of 27-inches, the blade itself formed into an acute curve. The first two-thirds of the blade design had a narrow width, while the last-third of its length (towards its point), called the Yalman: the blade flared, and was much wider. This feature was said to add to the swords' cutting power. The back of the blade had a distinct 'T-shaped' cross section that allowed for greater blade stiffness without increasing its weight. The distinctive shape of the blade around its tip allows a thrust movement to be performed, in addition to the typical sabre sweep-action, or slicing cut. The Kilij when compared to European sabres, it was said: "the edge of … [European] … sabres … [were] … never sharp enough, and the angle of the edge is too acute."[385] The Turkish weapon in comparison had a much thicker blade, with a broader edge. It is known, that Kilij:

> "have one great defect, brittleness; they are apt to fly like glass by a blow given injudiciously, though a person used to cut with them will, without any danger of breaking … or turning its edge, cut through an iron nail as thick as a man's finger."[386]

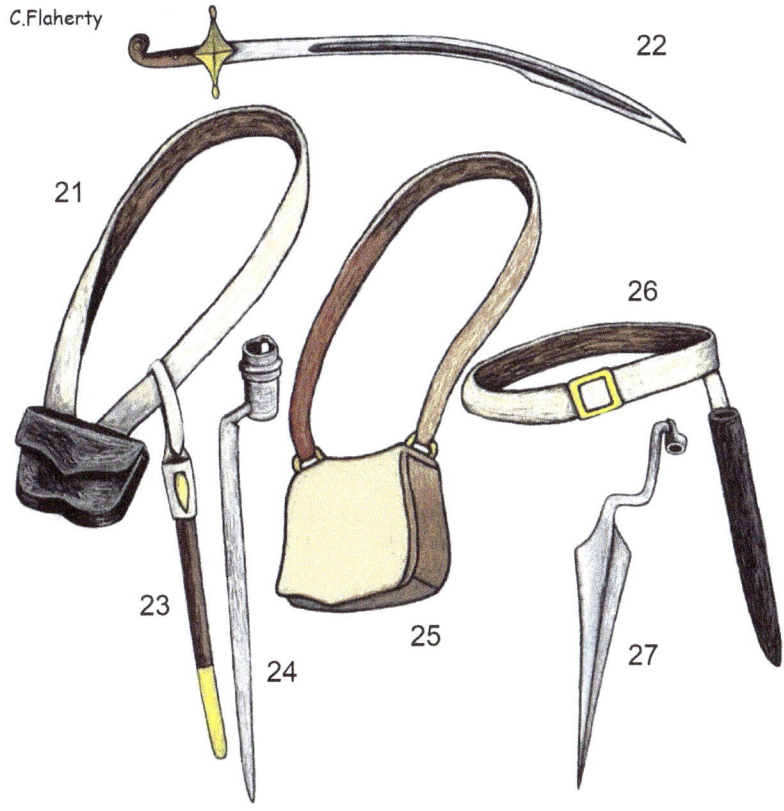

FIGURE 21: New Order Army cartridge box (1802).
FIGURE 22: Kilij: scimitar-sword.
FIGURE 23: 1777 Charleville musket bayonet scabbard.
FIGURE 24: 1777 Charleville socket bayonet.
FIGURE 25: Large ammunition pouch-box used by Artillery Drivers (late-18th Century).
FIGURE 26: New Order Army Soldier's waist belt and buckle, with bayonet scabbard attached.
FIGURE 27: Early Turkish bayonet used by New Order Army Soldiers.

---

384 Sevket, 1907.
385 Eton, 1798.
386 Eton, 1798.

CHAPTER 7: TOPCHEES: ARTILLERY AND NEW ORDER ARMY REGIMENTAL CANNON BULUKS: COMPANY

Traditionally, the Topchees: Artillery organization consisted of the following units and number of Gunners:

| Cemaat: Artillery Regiment | 250 |
| Boluk: Files: Artillery Sub-Regiments | 100 |

The Topchees flag, from the late-18th Century, was a small red banner with a pointed tail, and had a wide yellow boarder. The red field displayed a yellow cannon barrel and four cannon balls[387]. The banner was carried on a yellow staff, with a spear point finial. Like Janissary, each Artillery Regiment had its own Kazan: cooking pot, and was set up in similar fashion to Janissary, and played a similar role[388].

SAHI: LIGHT TO MEDIUM CANNON

Traditionally, the Sahi cannon category included a light version firing shot ranging between 150 grams, to 1.8-kilograms, or larger rounds: 4- and 6-kilograms: 3- and 5-okka (a Turkish weight measurement), respectively: light 2- to 13-pounder cannon. Sahi cannon had a distinctly long barrel[389]. It is known that from 1782 till 1789, carriages used for the Sahi cannon, were identical to that used by Speed Maneuver Artillery[390].

BALYEMEZ: HEAVY CANNON

A 1798 Turkish description, and drawing of a limbered, "Dessein de Gross Canon: large cannon design[391]; also known as the, "old Balyemez or Cannon de Batterie": Gun of Position[392]. It is calculated the barrel length was about 3.5 meters: 11½ feet long, and judging from the approximate diameter of the cannon ball this large piece must have fired shots of some 27- to 35-kilograms in weight[393]. This would be the equivalent of a 59½ to 77-pounder cannon. As early as the 1638 Ottoman siege of Baghdad it is known that 50-, and 70-pounders were used[394]. It is also known, generally the Ottoman 25-okka: 70-pounder or greater were used in sieges[395]. The Balyemez barrel immense weight was likely the reason for use of solid wheels, and axels made of solid iron, and heavy single block trail carriage with heavy bolted iron bands for added strength[396]. A 1732 illustration depicts two types of solid wheels, one is a flat type made of several pieces, bolted together with iron straps. A type of solid barrel wheel is also shown, said to be used to reduce the cannon height, but could also have been used for transport over soft surfaces, relying on the wide surface area to displace the

---

387   Sevket, 1907.
388   Raif, 1798.
389   Agoston, 2005.
390   Sakul, 2011.
391   Raif, 1798.
392   Agoston, 2005.
393   Agoston, 2005.
394   Sakul, 2013.
395   Nolan, 2008.
396   Marsigli, 1732.

weight of the gun. This would have required a modified long iron axel. A 1798 Balyemez illustration depicts a solid flat wheel with an iron rim, and six strengthening spokes, now on a double trail carriage[397]. The wheel diameter is 5 feet across. The wheels were secured with a hooked spike placed through a locking ring at the end of the axel. The most surprising aspect to the Balyemez carriage trail was its highly ornamented end, with either carved wood, or cast-iron floral leaves scroll.

The 1798 Pamphlet also depicts, "[a] … newly invented large cannon"[398]. The barrel was approximately 9 feet: 2.7 meters long. The carriage was similar to standard late-18th Century European heavy cannon field carriages, however the wheels like the larger Balyemez were Turkish solid types. Like the 1732 barrel wheels, the new cannon carriage had a small diameter, some 3⅕ feet: 97 centimeters across. The 1732 commentary stated:

> "[I] … having asked them why they make such wheels, they replied that it was in order to avoid having to raise the Batteries high. In fact, this use would not harm us in places."[399]

The wheels were strengthened with large iron cross braces, and had a convex shape, coming to almost 1 foot: 30 centimeters thick at the center.

BALYEMEZ AND NEW LARGE CANNON LIMBERS

The Balyemez carriage was provided with a long side handlebar, as the barrel had no handles, the side bars were the only attachment point for crane-lifting, or maneuver ropes. Balyemez was transported with its trail resting on a simple limber consisting of an axel block connected to a pair of wheels. A pair of long poles controlled a braking system. Traditionally, Balyemez cannon were the, "largest piece in the … arsenal ... [and] … was hauled overland by twenty pairs of buffalo"[400]. The carriage for the 1798 newly invented large cannon was a conventional French heavy cannon limber with smaller 3 feet: 91 centimeters diameter solid wheels.

▼ Balyemez limber wheels.

397	Raif, 1798.
398	Raif, 1798.
399	Marsigli, 1732.
400	Fleet, 2006.

▶ A 1798 Balyemez cannon, and solid wheel (and profile) for the newly invented large cannon.

SUR'ATCIS: SPEED MANEUVER ARTILLERY

The Sur'atcis [Suratci Ocagi]: Rapid-Fire Field Artillery Corps[401]; which more accurately was known as Speed Maneuver Artillery; or, "Mobile Field Artillery"[402]. The unit was originally formed in 1772, or 1774[403], and was mostly French trained under Baron Francois de Tott[404]. The unit was recorded as still existing in 1775, possibly as late as 1781, till 1782 when the French were recalled[405]. The force over this time had increased to 2,000 Soldier-Gunners.

It is known that regulations for the Speed Maneuver Artillery, "describe its ... distinct uniforms"[406].

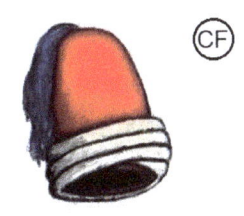

Little is known about the uniform except the Soldier-Gunners were, "identified by special uniforms and prohibited civilians from wearing the same garb."[407] Two similar figures are known, one is part of a 1907 set of uniform illustration under, "Regne du Sultan Abdul ... [Mahmud II] ... Avan l'Introduction de l'Uniforme Europeenn": before the introduction of the European uniform, described as Soldat d' Artillerie: Artillery Soldier[408], and is shown wearing a green button fronted jersey-jacket with a low collar edged in red tape, with a line of red tape running down the front with a line of small white buttons. A yellow and red striped waist sash, blue Russian pants and red Turkish slipper-shoes are worn. A long black open sleeveless coat, with outside hanging sleeves, is edged with yellow tape, and three pairs of red rosettes, with long tassels are placed on the coat flaps. The figure wears a tall domed red bonnet, with tassel on top, with a white turban. The other version is called an Artilleur-a-Cheval: Horse Artillery Soldier[409]; and has the following differences: The black over coat has a low collar edged in red tape, and its lining is red. The green collarless jersey-jacket sleeves are red, with more elaborate yellow embroidering around the neck, and down the button front. The turban, and waist sash appear red and yellow striped. Black Turkish slipper-shoes complete the dress.

An Artilleur-a-Cheval: Horse Artillery Soldier, from a black and white illustration, titled in full: Troupes Regulieres Turques – Artillerie[410]. The Artilleur-a-Cheval: Horse Artillery Soldier may be earlier, and date to the Sultan Selim III Era, than the rest of the figures depicted in the group – as these appear to relate more to the 1826 Era, under Sultan Mahmud II.

▲ Soldat d' Artillerie: Artillery Soldier (around 1750s), or Artilleur-a-Cheval: Horse Artillery Soldier (Sultan Selim III Era).

401	Aksan, 2007.
402	Aksan, 2002.
403	Nicolle, 1998.
404	Tott, 1786.
405	Nicolle, 1998.
406	Aksan, 2002.
407	Levy, 1982.
408	Sevket, 1907.
409	Brindesi, 1850.
410	Unknown, 1830.

The Artilleur-a-Cheval: Horse Artillery Gunner, figure appears to demonstrate a distinct French influence (from the 1796 Mission, or earlier), wearing what has been interpreted to be (from the original ink drawing), a large lace cravat. The original drawing appears to show the cuffs rolled back, revealing a more tight-fitting pointed cuff, from an inner sleeved coat. Depicted wearing a low collared bolero jacket with square ended fronts, with massively embroidered patches covering the shoulders, elbows, and front corners. The figure wears a tall soft bonnet, with a pompom on top, and tightly rolled striped turban, with three coils. A wide waist sash, Russian pants, and Turkish riding boots with large, decorated tongues hanging from the tops complete the dress.

An 1820 illustration of a Canonnier: Gunner[411], shows a figure wearing a light blue open bolero jacket with square-ended front flaps, edged with black tape. Two black tape cuff-rings, and black tape (edged in black dragons' teeth) shoulder wings are also seen. Light blue Russian pants appear tightly buttoned up the inside calf, and the ends edged with black tape. A yellow shirt has a broad black tape running up the center with white buttons, with decorative pairs of black crescents on either side. The waist sash is light blue, and the light blue bonnet has a white tuft, and a white turban with black and white crisscrossed lines on it. Yellow Turkish slipper-shoes complete the dress. Another Gunner, identified in an 1850 illustration as a, "Artilleur-a-Pied": Foot Gunner[412], likely dating to the Sultan Selim III Era, appears to wear a purple-grey open bolero jacket with square-ended front flaps. The waist sash is white with red lines. A red shirt has black lace decorations on it. The top hat is red, with a large black tuft on top, and a white turban with a long fringe. Purple-grey Russian pants, and red Turkish slipper-shoes complete the dress.

POST-1805 FIELD ARTILLERY

Artillery underwent significant development in the Napoleonic Period. By 1789, some 300 French Artillery Officers and Engineers were active in the Ottoman Empire modernizing and training Artillery. The French Revolution saw a continuation of Franco-Ottoman relations, and Sultan Selim III, turned to France to modernize, and reform the military. In 1796, General Aubert du Bayet with his Military Mission arrived at the Ottoman Court with Artillery equipment, bringing a set of new French Army light field cannon, which appear to have been Gribeauval system six-pounders. Under Sultan Selim III, Topchees, "in 1796 had 2,875 Cannoneers in 15 Companies of 115 Officers and Soldier-Gunners."[413] The major reform of the period was the creation of a Cannon and Howitzer Regiment-Brigade. Field and heavy cannon were manned by the Topchees, the Abus [Obus]: howitzer weapons manned by the Humbaraci: Bombardiers.

The main armament was the 1790 French designed Surat Topcusu: six-pounders. The cannon-type originally used for the Speed Maneuver Artillery was a four-pounder: Surat Topu, from 1768 till 1774[414]. In 1790, a French designed version appeared, and this was a six-pounder measuring about ten feet from the tip of the barrel to the end of the trail[415]. The Turkish-French designed 1790 Surat Topcusu cannon was not a true copy of the French Army's Gribeauval system six-pounder. Illustrations of the French designed 1798 cannon show that it more conformed to Prussian Artillery Drill Regulations, with the absence of an ammunition box placed between the carriage trails, as this was moved instead to the specially designed limbers[416]. The 1790 Surat Topcusu cannon were brigaded into the same Artillery Regiment with traditional Turkish designs, namely the Balyemez: heavy cannon, Sahi: light cannons, and Abus [Obus]: howitzer. From 1796, Regimental allocation of cannon[417]:

---

411 Unknown, 1815.
412 Brindesi, 1850.
413 Aksan, 2002
414 Sakul, 2011.
415 Johnson, 1997.
416 Raif, 1798.
417 Nicolle, 1998.

CANNON-TYPE	NUMBER	CANNON-TYPE	NUMBER
Surat Topcusu	Four	Sahi	Two
Abus [Obus]: Howitzers	Two	Balyemez	Two

From 1805, Artillery for the Field Army was standardized according to five different cannon calibre types: Turkish Cap-sizes[418]. The Ottoman 'Cap': indicated the weight of the projectile fired in okka:

Nine-Cap: Diameter	11.6-kilograms shot	25½-pounder
Seven-Cap: Diameter	8.98-kilograms shot	19¾-pounder
Five-Cap: Diameter	6.41-kilograms shot	14¼-pounder
Three-Cap: Diameter	3.85-kilograms shot	8½-pounder
1.3-Cap: Diameter	1.92-kilograms shot	4¼-pounder

One noticeable design difference incorporated into Turkish-French designed 1790 Surat Topcusu, shown in 1798, was addition of four iron pulling bars, and cross-rails that extended out from the front of the carriage – likely to ease handling and moving around[419]. The 1798 Pamphlet illustration shows the top-down view of these, showing these as large and prominent features. Pulling bars were fixed to the axel and the carriage wall side extending out as far as the wheel rim. An 1848 painting of a Turkish field cannon shows what appears to be a cast iron square-box axel directly bolted to the under-side of the double trail carriage[420]. This illustrates earlier Turkish designs, seen in 1732[421], and 1798 Pamphlet illustrations[422].

CARRIAGE LIVERY

Sultan Selim III, "accepted the color of yellow as the standard for the carriages and the ammunition carts in the aftermath of the war with the Habsburgs."[423] Following the Austrian model ironwork was finished in black.

AMMUNITION LIMBERS (CANNON WAGONS)

The French design 1790 limber carriage for the Surat Topcusu[424], resembled light cannon limbers commonly seen in Russian, Prussian and Austrian Armies of the period, rather than the typical French Gribeauval system. The 1790 Turkish-French limber carriage did not follow the Gribeauval system, as there was a 24-round ammunition box built into the seat of the carriage. The reason for this design difference, was that in 1793, Sultan Selim III ordered the adoption of the Prussian drill system for Artillery[425]. The effect of using the Prussian drill, loading crews went to the limber for ammunition, whereas in the case of the French, was in an ammunition box carried on the carriage, which had to be removed, allowing the cannon to be unlimbered and fired. In 1798, the ammunition wagon is illustrated showing a design based on French caissons of the period[426].

A 1788 dated illustration of the limber horse seen in Turkisch Kaiserliche Artillerie: Turkish Emperors' Artillery[427], shows blue square saddle cloths, edged in red. Red bridles, complete with a red

---

418	Sakul, 2011.
419	Raif, 1798.
420	Szatmary, 1848.
421	Marsigli, 1732.
422	Raif, 1798.
423	Sakul, 2011.
424	Raif, 1798.
425	Johnson, 1997.
426	Raif, 1798.
427	Unknown, 1788.

forelock knot, light tan colored neck boards, with white sheepskin hand rests, completed the set of horse equipment. The limber is not shown, except for the poles attached to carry straps on the horses' sides, indicating this is a typical 18th Century single horse limber, for light and medium cannon. An account from the English diplomat who accompanied the Turkish Army in Egypt, recorded seeing: "ten horses to draw a six pounder the distance of two miles, where a fresh relay relieved the first."[428] It is known that one of the problems faced by the Turkish Artillery in this period, was the heavy construction of the basic gun carriage, which were over-weight by contemporary European standards; so much so: "Horses had to be changed every 3-4 hours instead of eight which was the norm in Europe as they are exhausted by the cumbersome Artillery."[429] The main problem was that Turkish field cannon and carriages, "lacked adequate mobility because they weighed twice as much as their French equivalents."[430]

▼ Artillery Driver (1798).

428 Morier, 1801.
429 Sakul, 2011.
430 Sakul, 2013.

▼ The 1790 Turkish-French Artillery Limber Carriage.

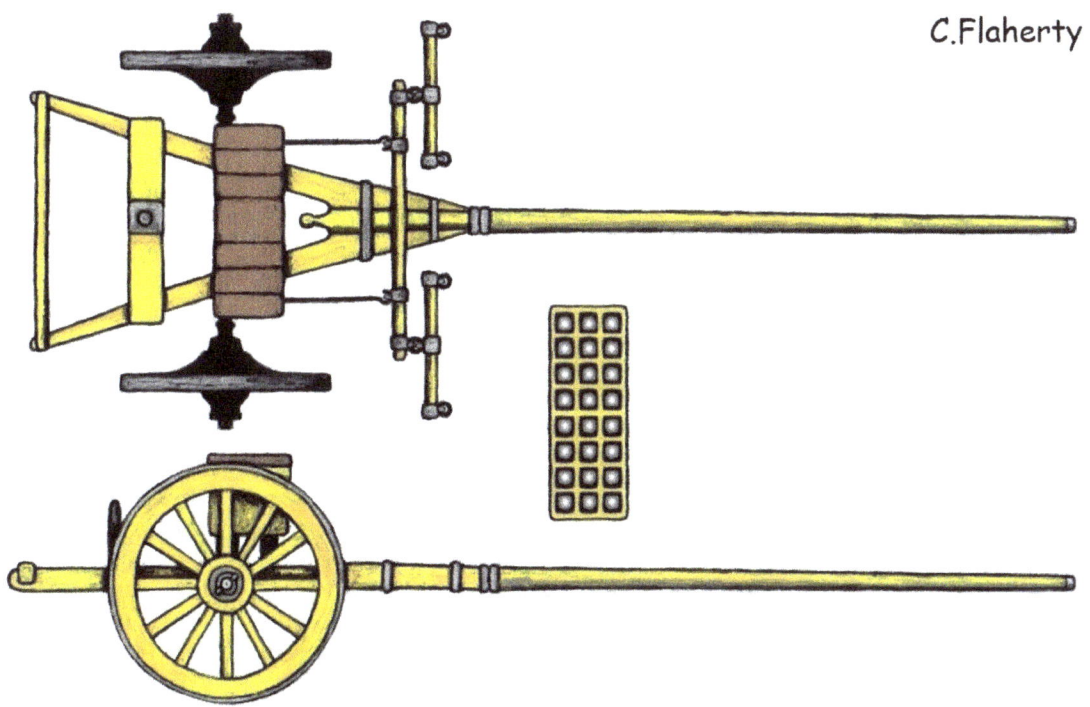

ARTILLERY TACTICS

Turkish 18th Century Artillery deployments were known to interspace mortars, in much the same way as howitzers were employed, between every three to four field cannons. This formation is illustrated in a 1721 painting[431]. Generally, Turkish Artillery tactics show a Battery of nine or more field guns deployed within a single large Brigade forming a Positional Battery[432]. The Guns of Position Battery is one of the older military terms describing a specific role for heavy fieldpieces, not designed for quick movements. The concept arose during the 17th Century, with the practice of Generals dragging a collection of various cannons into battle to serve as Guns of Position for, "preliminary bombardment of the opposing army"[433]. The Guns of Position as a military concept emerged in the period of the English Civil War (1642 till 1651), referring to the heavy cannon that were placed in static positions on a battlefield[434]. Under Louis XIV (1643 till 1715), use of the heavy Guns of Position was established as a common practice, placing these within protective field fortifications. In 1759, Frederick the Great, established heavier Guns of Position, which were dragged by horses in single file, led by civilian drivers on foot, and were generally formed in four masses, in the center, wings, and reserve[435].

The general practice was for the Turkish, "[to commence their] … attack with a discharge of Artillery"[436]. Many accounts suggest Artillery fire could be quite ineffective, such as at the battle of Heliopolis, in 1800, where Turkish Artillery till it was captured performed poorly: "The cannonade … balls … ill directed, flew over the heads of the … [French] … while … [Turkish] … Artillery was

---

431 Cavuszade, 1721.
432 Topkapi, 1609.
433 Dastrup, 1992.
434 Henry, 2005.
435 Hubert, 1911.
436 Anthing, 1813.

rapidly dismounted by the well-directed fire of their adversaries"[437]. Paintings and illustrations of Turkish cannon lines show only a few individuals working a larger number, rather than the more familiar crews of four, or five, or more working each cannon. The explanation for this lack of Gunners is that they tended to shelter directly behind cannon, as these were fired by an individual Gunner in quick succession[438]. This would lead to a situation where all the cannons, were reloaded at once, push back into line, to compensate for the inevitable recoil of the weapons themselves, which may have been reduced due to the practice of linking a heavy chain from one axel-hub hook to the next, creating a barrier with the cannons.

By the Napoleonic Period, even though there were four different cannon types allotted to the same Regiment, on the battlefield these units were functionally split up, as older Balyemez, and to a lesser extent Sahi cannons were extremely heavy and bulky, and usually kept in trenches at some distance from the actual fighting, treated as a type of Positional Battery'[439][440]. Sahi lighter cannons were organized into Mobile Batteries, likely of some five cannons, or less, along with the newer French cannon, and lighter Abus [Obus]: howitzer, as these pieces were quick enough to keep up with Infantry, and were often placed in the thick of battle'[441]. A European commentator, noted:

> "The Turkish Artillery was long superior to that of the European powers; and although it had not kept pace with the progress of Western science, and had sunk from its former celebrity during the wars of the Eighteenth Century, yet it was still formidable from the great number of guns which their armies brought into battle, and the rapidity with which their admirable horses moved them from one part of the field to another."[442]

NEW ORDER ARMY REGIMENTAL CANNON BULUKS: COMPANY

Infantry fighting from their cannon lines was well established in the 16th Century, and is often illustrated[443]. According, to an account from Egypt in 1800, Turkish practiced moving Infantry and Artillery attacks:

> "The Infantry and Artillery were drawn up in three bodies, that is, a main body and two wings, nearly in a line, with … [cannons] … in front. While the whole advanced slowly, a firing was kept up exclusively by the Artillery; and the movement having been continued for the space of six or seven hundred yards … During the whole of the time the Infantry remained with their arms shouldered"[444].

A 1788 illustration of the Turkish Army arriving at Sophia, Bulgaria, shows an almost identical maneuver, where ahead of each Infantry column a cannon is being handled forward[445]. In the Napoleonic Period, using Artillery Infantry to protect cannons, was a continuation of a traditional role of the 16th, and 18th Cemaat Janissary Orta, both of whom used crossed-cannon badges, and who are known to have, "marched with the Artillery"[446]. Under the New Order Army organization, the Infantry and Artillery overlapped with the creation of Soldat Canonnier Fusilier: Soldier-Gunners[447]. Artillery Infantry formed a special Boluk: Squad, numbering some ten Soldiers assigned to each cannon as extra-Gunners, and as Infantry, who were to protect the cannon from attack[448].

437	Alison, 1842.
438	Topkapi, 1609.
439	Johnson, 1997.
440	Nicolle, 1998.
441	Johnson, 1997.
442	Alison, 1840.
443	Suleyman, 1526.
444	Wittman, 1803.
445	Hochenleitter, 1788.
446	Johnson, 1988.
447	Vivien, 1900.
448	Johnson, 1997.

Being directly deployed in the battle line,

> "naturally resulted in increased casualties so in 1796 each Battery was assigned an additional 20 Soldiers whose job was to defend the guns in the field. While they were primarily ... [Infantry] ... , they were also cross-trained as … [Artillerists] … so they could take over ... [from the] ... dead or disabled Gunners."[449][450]

Various Artillery Infantry Boluk may have formed part of a much larger establishment, as it is known from the 1826 till 1828 Mansure Army organization, under Sultan Mahmud II (that largely reinstituted the original organization of pre-1807 New Order Army), composing a separate Artillery Infantry Command. A distinction between basic Gunners, such as a simple Soldat: basic Soldier in the Line Artillery; and Artillerie Legere: Light Artillery, composed of Artillery Infantry, is known[451]. Both entities, having separate command structures:

TOPCU: ARTILLERY CORPS		CANNON INFANTRY	
Bin-Bachi	Major	Colonel Des Canonniers Fusiliers	Regiment Commander
Ynz-Bachi	Captain	Capitaine Des Fusiliers Canonniers	Captain
Porte-Etendard	Standard Bearer	Fusilier Canonnier	Sergeant
On-Bachi	Corporal	Soldat Canonnier Fusilier	Corporal
Simple Soldat	Soldier-Gunner	Artillerie Legere	Soldier-Gunner

A key part of the 1796 introduction of French training was the development of mobile medium field cannon as integrated Infantry support. There was one Battery of Horse Artillery, and one Regiment of Artillery, with Topchees: Artillery Gunners. The Regiment had a Buluks: Company of Soldier-Gunners for the 4-, 8-, 10-pounders. Cannons and crews were allotted to the New Order Army Regiment for its use; and, each Infantry Buluks: Company was given one cannon, eight Gunners, one Cannon Master, and five Cannon Wagon (Limber) Drivers[452]. The cannon used may have been lighter types. Typically, the cannon type used to support the Infantry Buluks: Company had to be sufficiently light to be manhandled forward, as the rest of the Soldiers moved. Typically, in the 18th Century, Battalion Artillery piece was a three-pounder. In the case of Turkish, it is described as a Top: cannon[453]. This could be referring to a class of cannon seen on Turkish ships, used as bow-chasers in the 17th Century; these were Top-i Yan Sayka. The cannon only fired a two-okka shot, approximately 1.2 to 2.5-kilograms ball; or the equivalent of a five-pounder[454].

GRENADE BADGE

An illustration of an, "Officiers des Canonniers": Artillery Officer, dated from 1832[455], is more likely a Soldier from the Training Battalion Period, as the illustration shows headgear, and dress close to other 1802 figures, which consists of a soft white pointed bonnet, ending with a pom-pom and tassel, which is combined with a white turban and black fringed shawl wrapped around the top. The figure wears a red wrap-around jacket with black tape zig zag trim on the shoulders and cuffs. A yellow waist sash, with blue Russian pants, which have been buttoned tight around the lower leg, and have black tape zig zag trim on the leg-ends, and yellow Turkish slipper-shoes complete the dress. A large yellow French grenade badge is displayed on the right breast. It may be a type of rank, or award insignia for proficiency, or marking them out as a member of the Infantry Artillery attached to an Infantry Regiment.

---

449   Johnson, 1997.
450   Nicolle, 1998.
451   Vivien, 1900.
452   Shaw, 1965.
453   Shaw, 1965.
454   Agoston, 2005.
455   Unknown, 1832.

ARTILLERY BUCKET

The Artillery bucket design for the 1798 Turkish-French designed light cannon are not known. However, the later 1848 design is, and this was an all-metal sponge bucket made of sheet iron with tapering sides[456].

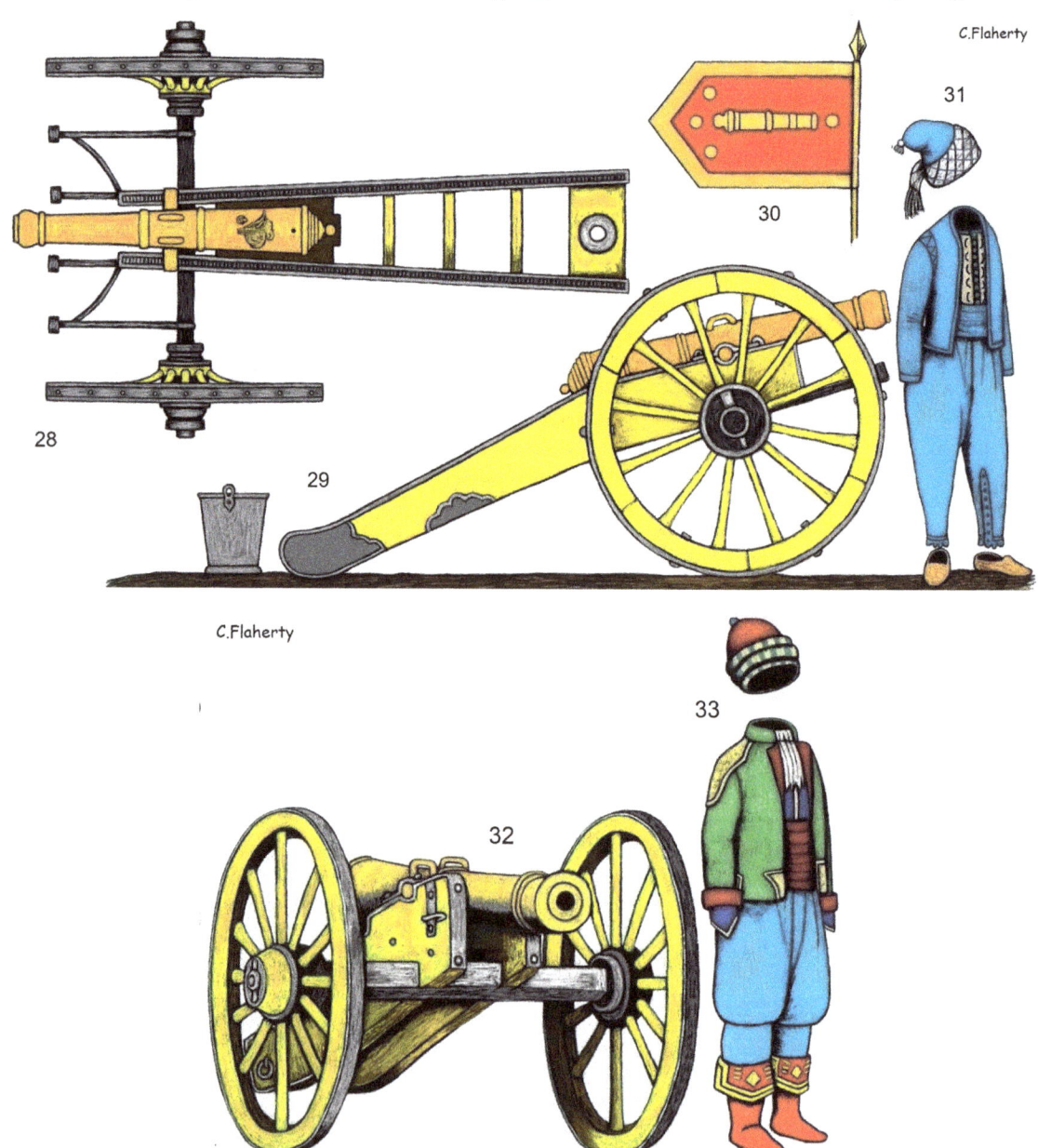

FIGURE 28: Top View - Turkish-French designed light cannon (1798).
FIGURE 29: Side View and metal sponge bucket (from later 1848).
FIGURE 30: Topchees flag (late-18th Century).
FIGURE 31: Artilleur-a-Cheval: Horse Artilleryman - Sur'atcis [Suratci Ocagi]: Rapid-Fire Field Artillery Corps (post-1798).
FIGURE 32: Later Era Turkish light field cannon, based on Napoleonic Period design.
FIGURE 33: Artilleur-a-Cheval: Horse Artillery Gunner, during French Mission (or earlier).

456   Szatmary, 1848.

CHAPTER 8: HUMBARACI: BOMBARDIERS

Humbaraci: Bombardiers manufactured mortars, howitzers, mines, grenades, and bombs. Humbaraci were divided into two departments; the first department were masters of cannon manufacture, and in the early-Renaissance had been able to construct, "mobile foundries", near the war front to cast mortars[457]. A possible description of mobile foundries operation is known:

> "were normally cast in one piece, according to eyewitness accounts, a gigantic and immensely strong mould with an inner core being placed muzzle downwards, and filled from the top with the molten metal from the adjacent furnace."[458]

The Humbaraci second department operated with Topchees: Artillery Gunners in the field, firing all the Abus [Obus]: howitzers and mortars. As well, Humbaraci crewed Ates Gemisi [Bomba Gemisi]: Bomb-Ketches in the Navy.

The Humbaraci banner, from the late-18th Century, was small with a pointed tail. It had a red field with a wide yellow border. The red field displayed a yellow mortar barrel[459]. The banner was carried on a yellow staff, with a spear point finial.

HUMBARACI ORGANIZATION

By the Napoleonic Period, Humbaraci organization consisted of five Regiments[460]. The 1st, 2nd, 3rd, and 4th Humbaraci Regiments were said to have been armed with ten mortars each. The 1st Humbaraci Regiment apparently operated a massive 65-centimeters (25½-inch) diameter mortar, which was more likely a typical Turkish bombard-mortar type of weapon. It should be noted that Dardanelles guns: great bombardes, or Kantar: stone firing cannon also fitted into this size category, and it may well be the case that this Regiment specifically operated these. Each Humbaraci Regiment specialized in a specific mortar size[461]:

1st	Stone Shot Diameter:	65-centimeters	25½-inch	500-pounder
2nd	Bomb Diameter:	36-centimeters	15-inch	400-pounder
3rd	Bomb Diameter:	22-centimeters	9-inch	70-pounder
4th	Howitzer Shell Diameter:	14-centimeters	5½-inch explosive bomb	

The 4th Humbaraci Regiment appear to have been armed with mortars that closely followed French and British 5½-inch weapons of the period. In addition, there appears to have been an emerging use of actual Abus [Obus]: howitzer, which may have been the five-inch type, organized as a Battery alongside the Topchees: Batteries, in the 1796 Cannon and Howitzer Regiment-Brigade. The 5th Humbaraci Regiment was armed with ten lighter Abus [Obus]: howitzer[462][463], in two different calibres:

Five Guns	Shell Diameter:	10-centimeters	4-inch explosive bomb
Five Guns	Shell Diameter:	7-centimeters	2¾-inch explosive bomb

Post-1807 Abus [Obus]: howitzer were represented by four calibres, measured in Turkish Cap-sizes, and fell into the range of 8-, 10-, 20- and 25-pounders[464]:

---

457 Sakul, 2013.
458 Losty, 1989.
459 Sevket, 1907.
460 Johnson, 1988.
461 Johnson, 1988.
462 Johnson, 1988,
463 Nicolle, 1998.
464 Johnson, 1997.

3-Cap: Diameter	8½-pounder	7-Cap: Diameter	19¹/₁₀-pounder
5-Cap: Diameter	14¹/₁₀-pounder	9-Cap: Diameter	25½-pounder

ABUS [OBUS]: HOWITZER

European Armies quickly adopted the Abus [Obus]: howitzer during the early-17th Century, following the 1635 introduction into the Dutch Army[465]. Early Dutch barrels were mounted on four-wheeled ship's carriages, that were used in the field. A museum model is known of a French 1691 9-inch field mortar barrel mounted on a cannon field carriage with a single-block trail[466]. A 1721 painting showing Turkish fighting the Polish Army[467], depicts mortars-howitzers (on Dutch four-wheeled ship's carriages) interspaced between two batteries of three, and four cannons. Barrels mounted on travelling carriages, based on cannon field carriages were adopted in most European Armies: Britain (1714)[468]; Prussia (1717)[469]. Howitzer barrels on cannon field carriages may have appeared quite late in the Turkish Army. A 1732 illustration shows a heavy bombard-howitzer type of barrel mounted on a sled carriage[470]. An 18th Century Turkish heavy howitzer barrel displayed in Paris, currently on a mortar bed from a later period, nevertheless reflects how it was originally mounted, due to its calibre[471]. The 1798 Pamphlet only depicts weapons that look like light howitzer barrels mounted on light mortar beds[472]. The design for a Turkish howitzer travelling carriage is not depicted. A British surgeon, with the Turkish Army in Egypt, recalled seeing Turkish Gunners practicing with Abus [Obus]: howitzers[473], but the carriage type is unknown. An account from the English diplomat, who accompanied the Turkish Army in Egypt, recorded: "the small train of Artillery, consisting of six-pound field pieces and five-inch howitzers."[474] It is not clear if he was referring to Turkish, or British weapons (as these had been supplied for the campaign), or a captured French weapon. It appears, this five-inch, which generally is a 12.7-centimeters weapon, was of a heavier type than the standard Abus [Obus]: howitzer used in the Turkish Army at the time.

MORTARS

In 1771, it is generally known the standard calibre mortars were 14-okka: 18-kilograms: 39¾-pounder; 18-okka: 23-kilograms: 50¾-pounder; and, 32-okka: 41-kilograms: 90⅓-pounder[475]. Historically, the larger ranging mortars were 85-okka: 104-kilograms: 229¼-pounder; to around a stone-shot 200-okka: 246-kilograms: 542⅓-pounder). Up to and including the 85-okka calibre mortar bomb shells were used, and the smaller mortars were used to fire grenades. A 1798 Pamphlet illustration shows the new light mortar design (which could be a howitzer barrel) resting on a flatbed base[476]. Regarding the lighter 5½-inch mortars, it is known that these were loaded five to a wagon[477]. Another 1798 Pamphlet illustration shows the heavy mortar was transported on its own wagon[478].

465	Art Institute of Chicago, 1635.
466	Musee de l'Armee.
467	Cavuszade, 1721.
468	McConnell, 1988.
469	Rogge, 2013.
470	Marsigli, 1732.
471	Musee de l'Armee.
472	Raif, 1798.
473	Wittman, 1803.
474	Morier, 1801.
475	Agoston, 2005.
476	Raif, 1798.
477	Johnson, 1988.
478	Raif, 1798.

HUMBARACI UNIFORMS

A figure called a Bonbardie: Bombardier Gunner[479], is part of a group identified as, "Regne du Sultan Abdul … [Mahmud II] … Avan l'Introduction de l'Uniforme Europeenn": before the introduction of the European uniform, and is shown wearing a yellow open bolero jacket with square-ended front flaps, edged with white wavy tape. The jacket is collarless, and sleeveless except for outside hanging sleeves. A white Turkish wrap-around collarless shirt with yellow stripes, and yellow Russian pants, which are usually tied-in below the knee, fitting close around the calves. The illustration shows decorative patches displayed below the knee on the front of the trouser legs, which suggests leggings are used. Leggings are commonly seen in Albanian dress. A Humbaraci tall black stovepipe hat, and red Turkish slipper-shoes complete the dress. A Humbaraci is depicted in an 1850 illustration Called: "Khoumbardji: Bombardiers"[480], and is shown wearing a green bolero jacket with square-ended front flaps, edged with thin black trim, with pairs of black cord chest lines, ending in tassels. The collarless buttoned shirt is white with red stripes. A red waist sash, and green Russian pants are worn with black trimmed green Albanian leggings, along with red Turkish slipper-shoes. A Humbaraci tall black stovepipe hat completes the dress. It is possible an additional green skirt, with black trim, open at the front, and covering the knees is worn over the pants.

Humbaraci Senior Officers are seen accompanying Sultan Mahmud II, at his Grand Review, on foot[481]. One figure is shown wearing a long blue coat, with a long-skirted pink collarless kaftan, with yellow Turkish riding boots, and a black spotted yellow waist sash completes the dress. The other accompanying Humbaraci Senior Officer wears a long sleeved open red coat with a light blue collar (matching the lining) over the shoulders. This displays two pairs of large chest buttons. A long-skirted pink collarless kaftan with gold tape trim and front closure buttons is worn with a blue and white striped waist sash, with pink Russian pants, and yellow Turkish slipper-shoes. Both wear the Humbaraci tall black stovepipe hat, used from the late-17th, and early-18th Centuries. Headgear was identical to that used by Deli Cavalry in the period. An early Napoleonic wars description of the tall headgear described these as a Tarturas, made of pasteboard and sheepskin[482][483][484].

(On the next page):
FIGURE 34: Humbaraci – Bombardier (Artillery specialist).
FIGURE 35: Humbaraci banner (late-18th Century).
FIGURE 36: Light mortar (or possible light howitzer) design (1798).
FIGURE 37: Humbaraci Senior Officer (up till 1810).
FIGURE 38: Humbaraci Senior Officer (up till 1810).
FIGURE 39: Light Turkish Abus [Obus]: howitzer (Napoleonic Period).
FIGURE 40: Humbaraci Bonbardie: Bombardier Gunner. Also showing Albanian legging details.

---

479   Sevket, 1907.
480   Brindesi, 1850.
481   Unknown, 1810.
482   Morier, 1801.
483   Wittman, 1803.
484   Tyrrell, 1910.

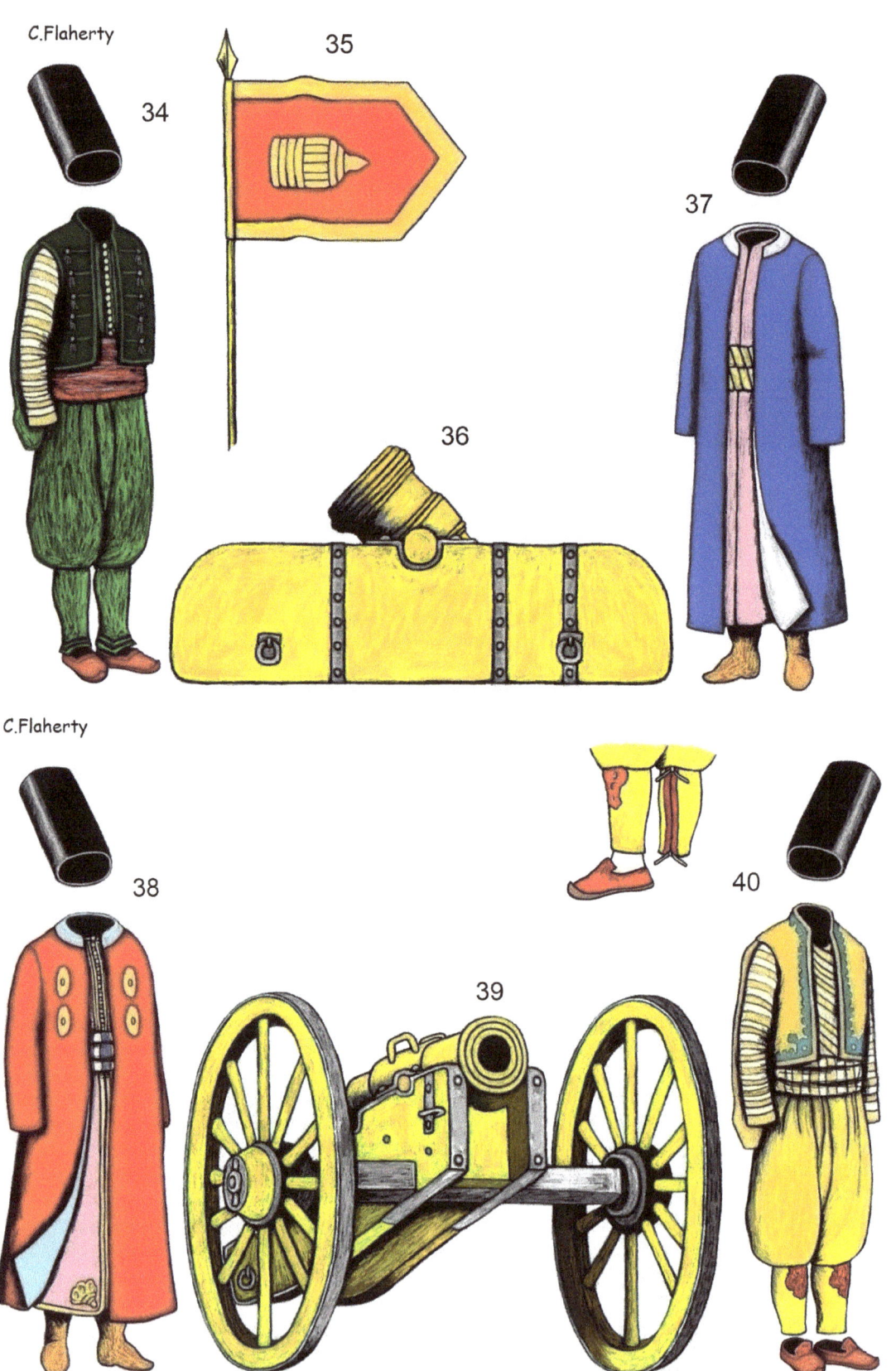

CHAPTER 9: ARNAUT INFANTRY

Arnaut: Albanian Infantry and Cavalry in the 18th Century were present in the Venetian Land Army across the Adriatic[485]. The Russian Army in the same period had, "Valakhian and Moldavian Arnaut"[486]. Valakhia [Wallachia], like Moldavia were Eastern Orthodox. Arnaut Infantry were counted among paid Government Soldiers, along with Janissary in the 18th and early-19th Centuries[487][488][489]. Arnaut Infantry appear to have been employed in large numbers, and in many cases could be Mounted-Infantry, or Dragoons: "several thousands of them … mounted during the last campaign in Egypt."[490] Like the Foot Soldiers, these were organized into Orta: Battalions, "some who are mounted, and several corps were so employed during the campaign in Egypt."[491]

MILITARY ETHOS, TRAINING AND ORGANIZATION

A 1770s Turkish Military Official complained Arnaut: Albanian Irregulars, "were … difficult to train."[492] A British diplomat who accompanied the Turkish Army into Egypt, in 1800 stated:

> "[The Arnaut] … are a warlike people, their only profession being that of arms … they find it much more advantageous to be paid for fighting: and they have become the mercenaries of Turkey, by hiring themselves to the different … [Pasha] … They retain much of the ferocity of the Spartans, of whom they are said to be the descendants"[493].

A 1798 survey, stated, "the Turks of Europe are the best Soldiers …. but far above all, those of Albania"[494]. Said to be: "the finest and best disciplined troops I had seen belonging to the Turkish Army."[495] They were also known as, "excellent marksmen, as well as very active in the field"[496]. Modern historians have noted:

> "Ottoman records described the Albanian Soldiers as brave, fearless, heroic, hard and warlike. Albanians served in the Army as Infantry and Cavalry. They were successful at the guerilla fights because of their lifestyles and for this reason they were chosen."[497]

A 1799 English travelers' description of an Arnaut Infantry Company, he saw in Damascus, seems to confirm distinctly European style of training: "a hundred and fifty Albanians, in uniform, and marching two and two, like our troops."[498] In line with their European training a British account describes how three Regiments of Arnaut Infantry, on landing in Egypt, "got British arms and accoutrements"[499].

It is known that the Albanian Infantry, "had a number of flags of different colors."[500] The tradition was to appoint a Bolukbasi: Sergeant, Standard-Bearer, and Non-Commissioned Officer to each group of 30 Albanian Infantry and Cavalry Soldiers, "apart from their leaders in order to command

---

485	Coralic, 2018.
486	Tooke, 1801.
487	Morier, 1801.
488	McLean, 1818.
489	Orenc, 2012.
490	Wittman, 1803.
491	McLean, 1818.
492	Aksan, 2007.
493	Morier, 1801.
494	Eton, 1798.
495	Low, 1911.
496	McLean, 1818.
497	Orenc, 2012.
498	Browne, 1799.
499	Low, 1911.
500	Low, 1911.

them easily" [501]. A Basbug: Chieftain was appointed to lead every 1,000 warriors[502]. Arnaut Infantry organization, during the Egyptian campaign, was described along similar lines to that seen among the Janissary Regiments, Segban Foot Musketeer or Levend Orta: Battalions: "[The Arnaut Infantry] … are usually formed into Orta: Battalions of 1,000 Infantry, under command of a … [Bimbashi: Chef de Bataillon]"[503]. In Egypt, in 1800, it was noted by another British observer that the Arnaut Infantry, were organized under: "A … [Bimbashi: Chef de Bataillon] … having under … [them] … several Officers of inferior ranks, commands a corps of these troops, a thousand strong."[504]

ARNAUT INFANTRY UNIFORMS AND CLASSICISM

An 1803 illustration of a Turkish Foot Soldier from the Egyptian campaign shows wearing an Cahouk: quilted top hat, with turban, short open red jacket, with yellow tape edging to the cuff-edge, and up the sleeve's back-seam, as well as wide blue breeches[505]. The figure is possibly a Levend Chiftlik Regiment, or Arnaut Infantry Soldier. A British account mentions the Arnaut Infantry uniform:

"[The … Albanians] … wore scarlet jackets, wide blue trousers tucked in at the knees, turbans and sandals on their feet"[506].

Illustrations show Arnaut Infantry wearing red trimmed green jackets, with fustanella: long-skirted shirt (which later formed part of Greek national costume)[507]. A Bensilan: traditional Balkan weapons belt, incorporating a belly wallet, for Yatagan: S-curved swords carried across the waist, along with pistols complete the dress. Another description stated:

"their dress would favor that supposition … [they descend from Spartans] … from its resemblance to the tunic … the fore part of the head, as far as the middle of the crown is shaved, and only a tuft of hair hang loose on the back part of the head, a red skull-cap of cloth comes far over their eyebrows, and gives them a very fierce look."[508]

Arnaut Infantry appear to have had a special distinction: "They wear a breastplate of silver, or white metal"[509][510]. The reference may be a ferahi: gorget[511].

◄ An 18th Century Harbadji [Hallebardier]: Halberdier in Sultan's Court dress, depicted wearing a scaled cuirass based on a classical Greek linothorax[512].

501	Orenc, 2012.
502	Orenc, 2012.
503	McLean, 1818.
504	Wittman, 1803.
505	Walsh, 1803.
506	Low, 1911.
507	McLean, 1818.
508	Morier, 1801.
509	Morier, 1801.
510	Wittman, 1803.
511	Eruretin, 2001.
512	Sevket, 1907.

An 18th Century example from the Sultan's Court, used by Security Officials, is a large silver plate edged with gilt metal, and displaying a gilt multipoint star and crescent badge. It is also the case, some Janissary in the 18th Century, as special court dress wore a scaled cuirass, made to resemble a classical Greek linothorax.

Arnaut Infantry are said to have worn: "in some cases cover the legs with a kind of armor, putting on sandals, to imitate in their dress, as nearly as they can, the Spartans, from whom they suppose themselves descended"[513]. Another description recalls Arnaut Infantry having a, "species of armor covering their legs"[514]. An 1818 dated illustration, originally identified as, "Officer of the … [Sipahi: Cavalry]", wear this type of metal leggings[515]. Arnaut Infantry were known to operate as Mounted Soldiers this may explain their identification as Sipahi: Cavalry; or these are specifically Arnaut Cavalry wearing the same type of legwear. Arnaut Infantry Soldiers' uniforms were clearly intended to have a classical Greek (or even Roman) appearance, as various styles of 'Roman sandals' with long crisscrossing straps, with metal decorations covering the calves are shown worn[516].

FIGURE 17: Turkish Foot Soldier in Egypt (1803).
FIGURE 18: A possible reconstruction of an Arnaut Infantry Soldier, wearing an 18th Century ferahi: gorget from the Sultan's Court.
FIGURE 19: Arnaut Infantry Soldier's Greek shoes' details (Napoleonic Period).
FIGURE 20: Arnaut Infantry Soldier (Napoleonic Period).

513	Wittman, 1803.
514	Morier, 1801.
515	McLean, 1818.
516	McLean, 1818.

CHAPTER 10: GALEONJEES: NEW ORDER ARMY MARINE REGIMENTS

The Galeonjees [Galangis; Galiondjis] were organized into two 500 Soldiers Regiments, in 1804[517]. It is known that these Marines in 1805, were possibly armed with rifled flintlock muskets[518]. The main Soldier force on Turkish warships were Galeonjees. Traditionally, they operated as a Soldier-Sailors' Corps, who provided all the military functions. Turkish warships' ordinary crew normally came from merchant sailors available in port for service on a ship, when it was to go out to sea. Traditionally, Galeonjees, were:

> "about 5,000 in number … [and] … permanently enrolled body at Constantinople of Seamen-Gunners and Seamen. The married men went to their homes at night, the bachelors lived in Barracks. They received each a ration, clothes, and about thirteen shillings a month. When a line-of-battleship, for example, fitted out, two master gunners, each with a crew varying from sixty to eighty men, a Bashrais (Boatswain) with a crew of about eighty men, a sailmaker and crew, were sent on board from the Galiondji Depot, with artificers from the dockyard."[519]

It is not known how Galeonjees were uniformed at this time. An 1800 account, from Egypt mentions, "a well-dressed Galangis, or Turkish Marine."[520] A post-1826 illustration of a, "Soldier of the Galeongees, or Marine Corps"[521], depicts a figure wearing a small red Fez, with a plain olive-green jersey-jacket, dark grey (almost black) Russian pants, and black Turkish slippers-shoes. A black cartridge pouch carry strap, and black waist belt with a plain open brass buckle complete the dress. The 1826 Mansure Army formed by Sultan Mahmud II wore uniforms not unlike the New Model Army Regulars, the only major difference was new types of headgear. It is supposed, small red quilted caps would have been used.

▲ Possible New Order Army Galeonjees' appearance (by the Author), and Kantar: stone firing cannon (1790 till 1810), on a ship's carriage.

---

517   Nicolle, 1998.
518   Shaw, 1969.
519   Slade, 1867.
520   Wittman, 1803.
521   Unknown, 1828.

CHAPTER 11: SAKA AND IMAM

The 1798 Pamphlet states Saka [Sakka]: Water-Distributor, "are uniquely distinguished by bronze belts and whips."[522] The traditional role was providing permitted: moving water for the Wudu Procedure: washing parts of the body required before prayers, and accompanying Soldiers into battle tending the wounded[523]. Saka also transported the Army's drinking water:

> "the Army has ... the establishment of ... [Saka] ... selected from the ... [Janissary] ... to attend and supply the troops with water. On this service they were also constantly employed on a march. They are mounted on horses provided with bells, to the end that their approach may be known to the troops; and each horse carries two leathern sacks containing about forty gallons of water."[524]

An 1802 description of the Saka noted: "It is a singular thing, that the business of a water carrier should afford a dress so ornamented"[525]. Napoleonic period descriptions list Saka as one of the Janissary Orta: Battalion Officers[526]. Saka carried a special leather water bottle, with a carry strap, brass reinforcement, and a small tap at the end[527]. A small brass handled pot used to transfer small amounts of water for ritual purification was held in one hand. The same pot is depicted in a 1714 illustration of a Saka and water transport horse, which shows a much larger version of the bottle slung over a saddle[528].

An 1812 dated illustration, titled: Topdjy Canonnier du Nizam Djedyd: Artilleryman of the New Order Army[529], is more likely a New Order Army Saka. Depicted holding a long handle rope whip, and wearing an open short pink jacket, with square-ended front panels edged with several large ball-buttons on both sides – which are likely to be bells, bell-jackets are also seen in a 1907 depiction of a, "Sakka (Porteur d'Eau)": Saka: Water Carrier[530]. A tall, red pointed bonnet, with a flat white wrapped turban is worn. A blue Turkish wrap-around shirt is also worn, with a belt closed by two square brass metal plates, with five ball decorations, connected by an S-clasp. Short blue loose pants closed around calves with buttons, and yellow Turkish slipper-shoes complete the dress. The 1714 illustration of the Saka, and their water transport horse, also shows a long handle rope whip, and wearing an open short jacket, with square-ended front panels edged with several large ball-buttons, or bells on both sides. Saka also used Tartavans: Turkish carriages suspended between two camels for carrying water[531].

The 1798 Pamphlet states: "Each Buluks: Company will have its Imam"[532]. All Janissary Orta: Battalions had their Imam[533]. The Janissary 94th Cemaat Orta: Battalion had a direct religious function. Commanded by a Chief Imam said to be the chaplain of all the Janissary Orta in Constantinople. The 84th Cemaat had an Orthodox Imam appointed[534]. The 99th Cemaat was commanded by a Seyk:

522	Raif, 1798.
523	Nicolle, 1995.
524	Wittman, 1803.
525	Dalvimart, 1802.
526	McLean, 1818.
527	Sevket, 1907.
528	Vanmour, 1714.
529	Castellan, 1812.
530	Sevket, 1907.
531	Wittman, 1803.
532	Raif, 1798.
533	Goodwin, 2013.
534	Goodwin, 2013.

Bektesi Dervishes Leader[535]. Also, "their Senior Baba (Spiritual Master) was honored as a Colonel of the 99th[536]. From 1591, eight Bektesi Dervishes attached to the 99th Orta on parade marched before the Agha of the Janissary in green uniforms[537]. A 1907 illustration of a Janissary Imam, dating from around 1750s onwards, shows wearing a long white low collared gown, with long red coat with wide yellow tape trim[538]. The Cahouk: quilted top hat is green, which traditionally, "denotes a man who has religious privileges"[539]. Yellow Russian pants, and red Turkish slipper-shoes complete the dress.

▼ Saka: Water-Distributors in the New Order Army (1798).

---

535   Nicolle, 1995.
536   Goodwin, 2013.
537   Gush, 1975
538   Sevket, 1907.
539   War Office, 2008.

CHAPTER 12: 1806 EDIRNE REBELLION

New Order Army Regulars fought three campaigns, beginning with participation by two Regulars Regiments quartered in Constantinople joining the Egyptian Expeditionary Force in 1799[540]. Organized into a French Battalion-size formation of 700 to 1,000 Soldiers, the Levend Chiftlik Regiment as it was called turned the tide in Acre's defence. Later, at the British fleet blockade of the French in Alexandria, some 2,000 Regulars landed along with 6,000 other Turkish troops, to maintain a successful blockade against the French at Rosetta, eventually forcing their surrender in April 1801. According to an 1878 history, it states how the Regulars – it identifies as Omar Aga's Corps, after Egypt,

> "further signalized itself by destroying some formidable bands of brigands or free companions, which had ravaged Bulgaria and Roumelia, and defeated the Janissary, whom the Pasha of those Provinces led against them. Sultan Selim III increased the number of new troops."[541]

In 1804, Kadi Abdurrahman Pasha's Regulars fought a campaign against Mountain Bandit Forces in the Balkan and Rhodope Mountains[542]. The Regulars marched against the bandits around Malkara (which is 61 miles: 99 kilometres from Corlu) on 28 July 1804, defeating them, while some of them escaped towards the Balkan Mountains[543]. As a conclusion to the 1804 campaign against Mountain Bandit Forces the Regulars' established a base in the town of Corlu.

1806 KADI ABDURRAHMAN PASHA'S MARCH

The 1806 Edirne (Adrianople) Rebellion, sparked by resistance to New Order Army recruitment in the city of Edirne, in northwestern Turkey, began in April, and throughout the summer. On 18 June 1806, the Regulars, under Kadi Abdurrahman Pasha[544], were ordered by Sultan Selim III to assemble in Edirne, intended for the city of Ruscuk, in Bulgaria, and for the defence of the Danube[545]. The task was to build additional Regulars' Barracks between Edirne and Constantinople[546]. Soldiers and recruits were called from all over Anatolia to the Uskudar Barracks. By 1806, about 16,000 all ranks of the New Order Army Regulars were in existence[547]. However, other sources suggest there were: 22,685 Soldiers, and 1,590 Officers in the New Order Army by this time[548][549]. The total force arose to 24,000 with Cavalry sent by Anatolian nobles: Karaosmanoglu and Capanoglu family dynasties. By 1806, a return of the Regulars, under Sultan Selim III's orders to establish more Barracks in Rumeli, to be quartered at Edirne (Adrianople), turned into the revolt of 1806[550]. The 1806 confrontation between Regulars and Rumeli Janissary, was result of Ayans: local nobles, fearing they would lose their field of recruitment, and that the Regulars' Army might become strong enough to end their independence[551]. It is said, that court conservatives' faction alliance in Constantinople led by Grand Vizier Hafiz Ismail Aga plotted to form an Ayans' Army from Edirne and march to Constantinople eliminating Sultan Selim III and the New Order Army.

---

540 Mugnai, 2022.
541 Creasy, 1878.
542 Mugnai, 2022.
543 Yesil, 2016.
544 Creasy, 1878.
545 Mugnai, 2022.
546 Yildiz, 2017.
547 Roubicek, 1978.
548 Shaw, 1965.
549 Aksan, 2007.
550 Mugnai, 2022.
551 Mugnai, 2022.

TEKIRDAG, CORLU AND SILIVRI

At the city of Tekirdag, located on the north coast of the Sea of Marmara, in East Thrace, there was violent opposition to the Regulars from the populace, when they arrived. City authorities refused to take part in establishing Barracks, and their replacements lynched by a mob after reading Sultan Selim III's edict. Tekirdag refused to admit the Regulars or turn over the killers. The Regulars set-up camp outside the city. A blockade from the sea, was organized by Turkish warships. Sultan Selim III sent orders for the Regulars to march to the town of Corlu, and the city of Silivri (located in a district in the Constantinople Province), where they met a similar civic response. Throughout the rest of spring and summer, local political opposition threatened to turn into an outright revolt. New Order Army Regulars were attacked along the route they relied on for supplies by rebels, who captured and murdered the Regular's Purchase Agent, killing Couriers, and seized monies that were to be used to buy the Regular's provisions. Kadi Abdurrahman Pasha's Regulars laid siege to the town of Babaeski [Babaeska][552], defeated the rebels, on the road of Corlu, seizing animals and grain supplies to feed the Regulars.

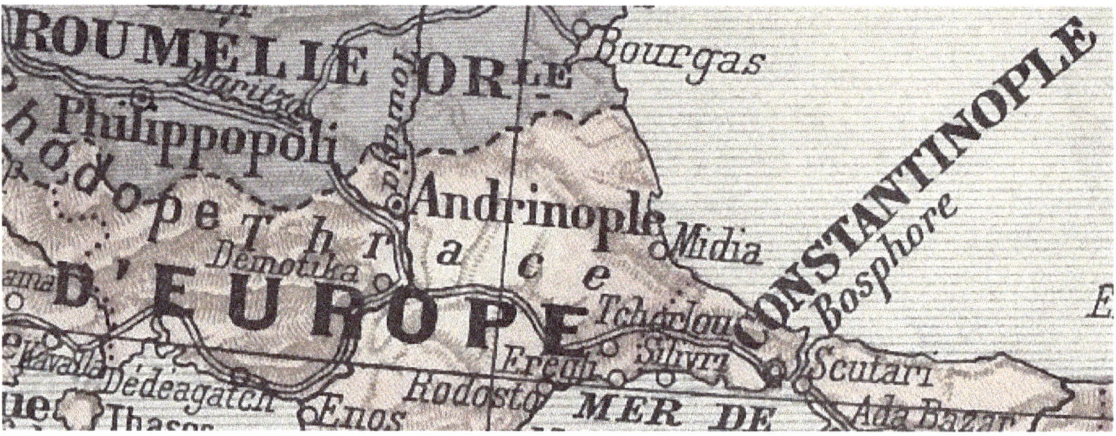

▲ Edirne (old Adrianople), and the city of Silivri, and town of Tchorlou (Corlu).

▼ The 1804 till 1806 New Order Army Regulars' Campaign map, and battle sites for Malkara (1804), and Babaeski (1806).

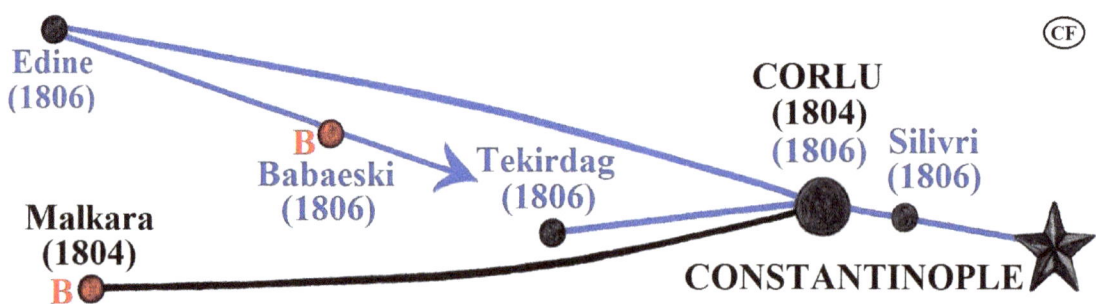

---

552   Kirca, 2010.

EDIRNE REBEL ARMY

A few days after 18 June, when Sultan Selim III had ordered the Regulars to assemble in Edirne, the influent Balkan Ayan Tirsiniklioglu Ismail [Osmail Tirsiniklioplu], at the Grand Vizier's secret urging, marched on Edirne with a Rebel Army estimated at some 80,000[553]. This force is said to have been collected by Rumeli Ayans: local nobles, and a coalition of Balkan notables. However, this may have been a ruse, which caused Sultan Selim III to delay sending Kadi Abdurrahman Pasha's Army against them[554]. The rebels repeatedly demanded disbandment of the Regulars. An 1878 history mentions that the force at, "Adrianople … gathered together in resistance to the Sultan's edict to the number of 10,000."[555] This was the actual force, organized by the Ayan of Edirne consisting at its core of the Rumeli Janissary, and Yamak[556]. Troops like Yamak: Auxiliary Levies[557], could at the time mean Janissary serving at the frontier forts[558]; it also could mean, "apprentice … recruited with the promise of enrollment in Janissary Corps if they served three years with distinction."[559] The Rumeli Janissary were largely 'Economic Janissary', who had come about through, "enrolment of Muslim artisans in the Janissary Corps … [that] … gave them status, including the right to bear arms."[560] Dress for the Rumeli Janissary was likely typical of most Turkish Volunteer Soldiers at the time:

> "The … [Volunteer] … takes a pair of richly furnished pistols (if he can afford it, for in the richness of their armour is their pride) a sabre covered with silver, and a carabine, and mount, his horse"[561].

> "All the Turks wear turbans, loose jackets, short pantaloons, morocco slippers, and a sash round the waist, in which they constantly carry a long dagger and a brace of pistols … Their heads are close shaved, and covered by a small scull-cap, which is hidden under the turban."[562]

The Edirne Rebel Army, incorporated troops derived from long-standing practices where Ayan and Janissary Agas hired gangs of brigands, mercenary Soldiers, armed Albanian mercenaries to terrorize and dominate the country[563]. The Rebel Army likely also included other Provincial Soldiers sent by local power holders at Havsa (a town in the Edirne Province of Turkey), and Irregulars belonging to several Brigand Leaders.

BATTLE OF BABAESKA

Kadi Abdurrahman Pasha's Regulars at the time of their battle with the Edirne Rebel Army, numbered some 15,000 to 20,000[564]. Finally ordered to confront the Rebel Army in mid-July, an 1878 history states, that Kadi Abdurrahman Pasha's Army of Regulars:

> "was intercepted at Babaeska on the Yena by a large force of Janissary and other troops opposed to the change of system. A battle ensued, in which the … [Regulars] … were utterly defeated." [565][566]

Babaeska [Babaeski] is only 17 miles: 28 kilometres from Havsa on the road between Edirne and Corlu. At that battle, it is said the New Order Army Regulars sustained considerable losses[567]. The

---

553 Mugnai, 2022.
554 Mugnai, 2022.
555 Creasy, 1878.
556 Mugnai, 2022.
557 Gokcek, 2001.
558 Yildiz, 2012.
559 Uyar, 2009.
560 Sadat, 1972.
561 Eton, 1798.
562 Walsh, 1803.
563 Sadat, 1972.
564 Aksan, 2007.
565 Creasy, 1878.
566 Gokcek, 2001.
567 Aksan, 2007.

reason for the loss is not clear. A later observation from 1807, about fighting between Janissary and the Regulars, the British Ambassador to the Porte, Charles Arbuthnot, described the fight that occurred between them in the streets of Constantinople:

"Janissary, it is true, were not sufficiently to be depended upon, either in point of obedience or training. Individually, however, they are expert in the use of the weapon to which they have been accustomed, and although they are very inferior to the disciplined troops of European powers, it is to be doubted whether they do not preserve some advantage over the Soldiers of the New Turkish Institution who have not yet been taught to act with confidence in a collective body, and whose mode of training must debar them from the separate feats of personal prowess by which the Janissary have ever been distinguished." [568]

Sultan Selim III capitulated after a series of bloody encounters between Regulars and Janissary in early August[569]. Retreating from their loss at Babaeska, the Regulars, "retraced their route to Silivri where they were halted by Sultan Selim III himself"[570]. Corlu, some 24 miles: 40 kilometres away, was besieged and successfully captured. On 19 September, Sultan Selim III, dismissed Kadi Abdurrahman Pasha, and ordered the Regulars to leave Silivri, and return to the Capital. The Edirne rebels were pardoned[571][572].

C.Flaherty

▶ A Janissary Imam (from 1750 onwards), and Volunteer Soldier, or possible Yamak (by the Author):

568 Mugnai, 2022.
569 Mugnai, 2022.
570 Mugnai, 2022.
571 Aksan, 2007.
572 Mugnai, 2022.

CHAPTER 13: THE 1807 END

Yamak: Bosporus fortresses Guards, were stationed at a string of Bosporus Forts setup against the rising Russian threat since 1785. The total number of Yamak was small, as the Bosporus Forts only accommodated some 1,500 Soldiers in 1807, and in May only 910 are recorded in returns.

Bosporus Fortress and Yamak Numbers in May 1807:			
Kilyos-Bagdadcik	205	Yusa Burnu – Macar Tabya	Not Known
Revancik	98	Telli Dalyan	Not Known
Rumeli Feneri	165	Anadolu Kavak	Not Known
Anadolu-Feneri	139	Rumeli Kavak	Not Known
Garipce	187	Kirecburnu	Not Known
Poyraz Limani	Not Known	Kilburnu	Not Known
Liman-i Kebir	116	**TOTAL**	**910**

Ordinary Yamak: locally recruited Garrison troops, were part of a rigid hierarchical system within the forts[573]. At the top of the military hierarchy was a Dizdar: Senior Officer of a Fortress (Commander); Kethuda: Subordinate of a Dizdar; and, Cebehaneci: Chief Artilleryman and Armourer.

On 25 May 1807, during the Yamak quarterly pay delivery, which had travelled by boat to Rumeli Kavak, the attending Aga, escorted by a company of Regulars, attempted to persuade the Yamak to accept New Order Army training and uniforms[574]. It should be noted, this account may not be entirely correct, as, "[archival sources leave] … no doubt that a group of … [New Order Army Regulars] … was stationed at the forts about two months before the uprising."[575] It is said, as the Aga started distributing new uniforms, the Yamak attacked and tore him apart[576]. Yamak chased and caught-up with the Regulars, who managed to escape by boat and land at Buyukdere. On the second day of the Yamak mutiny, Kabakci Mustafa, from the Rumelian fortress, said to be encouraged by Ulema: Religious Scholars, and Constantinople Janissary support, himself joined the revolt. The Bosporus Garrisons then refused to wear the Regulars' uniforms and joined the mutiny. Constantinople Janissary joined in the following days.

Yamak Soldier's dress is generally not known, and the consensus is they did not wear a uniform, given their lower status and poverty[577]. Usually thought-off as Auxiliary Levies, or apprentices, their clothing was likely close to Provincial Levend: Armed Militia. An 1805 illustration of a Leventi depicts a Soldier, armed with a heavy bore flintlock musket, and wearing a simple blue collarless shirt, with sleeves rolled-up[578]. The shirt has a wide orange patch running down the front, with many small black buttons. A red waist sash carries a knife, powder horn, and European hanger sword. Small grey turban, grey knickerbockers breeches, blue stockings and yellow Turkish slipper-shoes complete the dress.

---

573   Yildiz, 2012.
574   Mugnai, 2022.
575   Yildiz, 2012.
576   Mugnai, 2022.
577   Yildiz, 2012.
578   Unknown, 1805.

THE 1807 BAYONET CAUSE CELEBRE

The May 1807 Yamak revolt has been linked to a Janissary complaint that European training turned them into, "fighting like robots"[579]. This criticism appears to have been directly linked to the military principles of Frederick the Great, a system based on the absolutist concept, and insistence on exact discipline Army, that enabled him to form his conceptions in the knowledge these would be realized:

> "[this military system] ... accommodated the need of a King (or his General) to have at his disposal a mechanism by which he could see his ambitions realized. The ordinary Soldier was merely a machine through whom the King acted against his opponent."[580]

Janissary were said to be opposed to using the bayonet, which was likely more a cause celebre. Historically, it has been argued that throughout the late 17th, and 18th Centuries, "[Turkish] ... Soldiers ... rejected the use of the pike and ... [later] ... the bayonet as 'infidel arms', and their objection ... was expressed in cultural-religious terms."[581] In regards to pike use, it appears this weapon was initially used by Janissary in the age of Sultan Suleyman [Suleiman I] the magnificent (1520 till 1566). By the time of Sultan Mahomet IV (1648 till 1687) the Janissary, "had given up the use of the pike"[582]. There appears to have been two short-lived attempts to introduce bayonets, said to have been, "in 1738 ... then dropped and taken up again in 1755"[583]. Little is known about the use of these weapons except these were listed as part of the weapons of the Janissary from a stocktaking in the Museum of St. Irene, in Constantinople, and the dates coincide with known attempts at military reform[584]. The only image we have of a Janissary armed with a musket and bayonet, is that of the 1770 Polish Janissary[585]. The bayonet version differed markedly from typical European designs and was only seen illustrated with the first known picture of a New Order Army Soldier from around 1802[586][587][588]. Not adopting the bayonet was an issue of military debate in the mid-18th Century, and one well known French commentator, the Chevalier Folard, who:

> "attributed the defeats of the Turkish armies in the early part of the 18th Century almost entirely to their neglect in not availing themselves of the improvements ... in the weapons of war. In his opinion it was the bayonet that had given the Christians their victories over the ... [Turkish]."[589]

Late-18th Century bayonet drill was nascent, confined to only two motions, from resting shoulder position, to 'charge bayonets breast high', followed by the command, 'push bayonets', which was a driving action with the bayonet horizontally out in front of the Soldier[590]. In 1740, the Prussians changed the position adopting a new motion, which was universally adopted in European Armies, and was likely the basis of the bayonet art taught to Turkish Soldiers; namely holding the musket with its bayonet at waist height, this allowed a Soldier easier control over the weapon, and made it much easier to naturally parry, any opposing bayonet movements. Nevertheless, this was still a relatively restricted move, as Soldiers were typically packed into a dense mass, with each Soldier only occupying a file width of 24 to 30-inches each. The only additional development in this period,

---

579	Nicolle, 1995.
580	Flaherty, 1996.
581	Levy, 1982.
582	Creasy, 1878.
583	Brill, 1913.
584	Levy, 1982.
585	Le Prince, 1770.
586	Dalvimart, 1802.
587	Unknown, 1812.
588	Roubicek, 1978.
589	Creasy, 1878.
590	Nolan, 2008.

was that of the Russian General Alexander Suvorov, who during the latter 18th Century Russian-Turkish Wars, "taught ... [his Infantry] ... how to use the bayonet against the Turkish sabre."[591] Even with an element of bayonet skill, opposing Soldiers could still be overwhelmed, such was the case, at what was to be the final breach at the siege of Acre by French Soldiers, who were pushed back by the Turkish defenders: "the bravest amongst … [the French] … fell by the sabre and the poniard of the Turks, one in each hand proving an overmatch for the bayonet."[592] Another commentator, noted that Janissary were heavily armed, along with their bladed weapons, such that in a melee: "the European Soldier, with … [their] … musket and fixed bayonet, is placed under great disadvantage against an enemy so well armed both for attack and defence."[593] The 1798 military Motions for the New Order Army Soldiers, illustrate two orders associated with bayonet use in combat[594]; namely: hold the bayonet towards enemy Cavalry; and, bayonet towards enemy Infantry. Basic drill may not have been that extensive: "The new Soldiery are taught their exercise with the musket and bayonet, and a few maneuvers."[595]

▼New Order Army's Drill Regulations (contained in the 1798 Pamphlet)[596], show Soldiers' Motions 29 and 30 for bayonet fighting techniques:

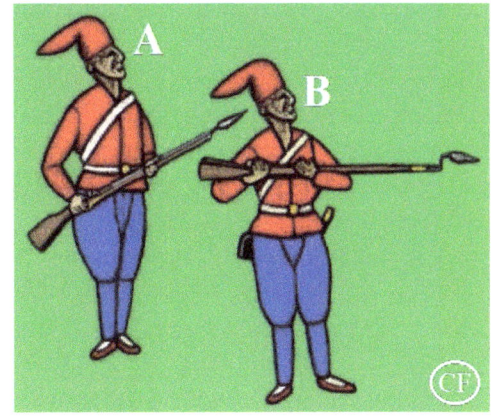

Figure A shows Motion 30: Croisez la Bayonnette vers l'Ennemi Cavalier: Cross the bayonet towards enemy Cavalry. Based on the 1740 Prussian stance, intended as a static defensive position.

Figure B shows Motion 29: La Bayonnette vers l'Ennemi Fantassin: Bayonet towards enemy Infantry. This motion is based on the original 'charge bayonets breast high'. This action appears to be conducted, while Soldiers push forward, with their muskets held high up the chest, not unlike the original use of the pike during an offensive advance.

Comparatively, Janissary traditionally fired their muskets, then at a certain point downing, or slung their firearms to facilitate a massed charge into the enemy fighting individually with their edged weapons. The tactic gave Janissary the opportunity to use their formidable sabre skills, and afforded engaging in the lucrative business of head-hunting for profit. In the 18th Century, it was believed only the: "[Turks] ... and certain crack troops ... had the elemental courage that was required to press home attacks sword-in-hand"[597]. In most cases, the extent of the use of the bayonet:

> "like an orderly advance in line was not unknown in the Age of Reason, but the well-authenticated instances are much rarer than might be supposed, and they are associated with specific circumstances ... [such as the fight for an entrenchment or some defended place]"[598].

Even in these special circumstances, the art of bayonet fighting as it existed at the time, had little in the way of formal mastery beyond - "Get stuck in, lad, or somebody will stick one in you!"[599]
Modern historians tend to view Turkish military conservatism in the 18th Century, in terms, "[of

591   Creasy, 1878.
592   Brenton, 1837.
593   Valentini, 1828.
594   Raif, 1798.
595   Eton, 1798.
596   Raif, 1798.
597   Duffy, 2005.
598   Duffy, 2005.
599   Duffy, 2005.

the] … stereotypes of religious obscurantism"[600]. In the case of the attempt by Sultan Selim III to mass introduce European drill,

> "[he] … found himself obstinately resisted not only by the … [Janissary] … but that powerful party in all the Ottoman Provinces who were attached to their national and religious institutions, and regarded the introduction of European customs, whether into the Army or the state, as the first step in their national ruin."[601]

> "the older corps in the past had demonstrated violent reactions to any attempts to introduce new ways which might undermine the position they had secured in Ottoman society by virtue of their monopoly of the military techniques and weapons of the past."[602]

Use of weapons, tactics, organization, and appearance of the Soldiers was infused with, "religious-legal sanction"[603]. Mandatory religious regulations underlay traditional military practices, to the extent that, "the Ulema … [Religious Scholars] … perceived any kind of advance or innovation as a direct attack on Islamic law and traditions."[604] Under Sultan Mustafa III, the 1774 order to establish a new corps of Speed Maneuver Artillery: Sur'atcis gave this official explanation, in religious terms: "Even though the Imperial Arsenal is known for its perfection in the arts of war … in recent times, other states have invented and developed small, well-crafted cannon capable of rapid fire, reaching an understanding of the science through experimentation … The Ottoman state likewise wishes to organize … Rapid-Fire Artillery … [Soldiers] … and is issuing this Imperial Order to that effect."[605] It has been argued, the reason why this explanation had to be given, was anticipation over the controversy generated within the Government and military establishment by introducing foreign military concepts, such as the adoption in 1774 of Flying Artillery based on European models. The edict of Sultan Mustafa III reflected Islamic teachings on the conduct of warfare that justified the adoption of a European Flying Artillery model, in accordance with the principle of Mukabele-i Bi'i-Misl: the permissibility of learning from one's enemy[606][607].

It appears, there was a substantial body of teachings laying down mandatory religious regulation for traditional uniforms, weapons and tactics. Mass destruction of Janissary materials after 1826 meant it is not known the extent, or in what form the religious regulations took. It is known these played a significant role:

> "Many acknowledge … [military weakness of the Turkish] … but … at the same time acknowledge their inability to effect a reform, which nothing but a change of religion could effect … [this] … prevents their taking any steps to security because the fate of the Army is supposed to be decreed … [by the will of God]".[608]

Deep connection between religion and military reform lay at the core of the political chaos of 1807, where it is said:

> "Emissaries from the Janissary … unknown to the … [Sultan] … mingled in … [the ranks of the New Order Army Regulars] … the powerful body of the Ulema … [Religious Scholars] … began to preach insurrection upon the ground of the … [Sultan] … aiming at the overthrow of the fundamental institutions of the Koran and the Empire"[609].

600	Aksan, 2002.
601	Alison, 1842.
602	Shaw, 1965.
603	Levy, 1982.
604	Mazanec, 2016.
605	Aksan, 2002.
606	Levy, 1982.
607	Sakul, 2012.
608	Morier, 1801.
609	Alison, 1840.

NO! TO THE EUROPEAN HAT!

During the 1808 continuation of the political unrest, the Janissary revolt facing short term reversal of fortune, apparently attempted to plead for royal mercy claiming they would adopt the New Order Army uniforms, and even the, "European hat should the Sultan demand."[610] Turkish commentators, at the time, criticized this political maneuver on the grounds,

> "[this] … was a scandalous idea since wearing the European hat amounted to changing one's identity. It demonstrated that the rebels had doubtful religious convictions; they would turn infidel"[611].

The reference to a 'demand by the Sultan to wear a European hat' may be pointing to the clothing laws implemented under Sultan Selim III in this period[612]. The question as to what is supposed to be the 'European hat', worn by the New Order Army Soldiers, has not been identified. The only item of clothing coming close was the French blue beret, said to have been worn by the Levend Chiftlik Regiment[613].

Sultan Selim III's Clothing Laws were used to compel compliance with his reforming policy direction for society. It may well be the case that the actual source of military opposition to his rule had been over reforms to the dress and appearance rather than the 'bayonet cause celebre' in 1807. Janissary uniform in this period only consisted of three items - Bork: hat, breeches, and boot color. Bork: hat was the primary means by which individual's status and role was known. The replacement of the elaborate headgear, used within the military, such as the Janissary bork: hat with a common 'European hat', would have meant a personal loss of status to the wearer, and fundamentally undermined any religious meaning or significance this may have had. For the back flap or tail on the bork: hat is said to represent the arm sleeve of the early Turkish spiritual leader - Haji Bektash (1209 to 1271), who named and consecrated Janissary, giving them their special role in society, when he is said to have placed his hand of authority on the first Janissary heads[614].

RESTORATION AND ASSASSINATION

The brief restoration of Sultan Selim III and assassination, in 1808 saw enthronement of Sultan Mahmud II. In 1807, about 2,000 New Order Army Regulars took part in the campaign against the Serbs[615]. During the Russian-Turkish War (1806 till 1812) some 4,000 Regulars filled the ranks of the Army until 1808[616]. These were likely from the Segban Provincial Militia Reserves – representing four Musketeer Regiments.

610	Sakul, 2012.
611	Sakul, 2012.
612	Quataert, 1997.
613	Shaw, 1965.
614	McLean, 1818.
615	Mugnai, 2022.
616	Mugnai, 2022.

REFERENCES

Agoston, G. 2005 Guns for the Sultan: Military Power and the Weapons Industry in the Ottoman Empire. Cambridge University Press.
Agoston, G. 2011 Military Transformation in the Ottoman Empire and Russia, 1500–1800. Kritika: Explorations in Russian and Eurasian History. Volume 12.
Aksan, V.H. 2007 Ottoman Wars 1700-1870: An Empire Besieged. Routledge.
Aksan, V. 2002 Breaking the Spell of the Baron de Tott: Reframing the Question of Military Reform in the Ottoman Empire, 1760-1830. The International History Review. XX. Volume 2 (June).
Alison, A. 1842 History of Europe from the Commencement of the French Revolution in 1789, to the Restoration of the Bourbons in 1815. Volume 2. New York: Harper & Brothers.
Alison, A. 1841 History of Europe from the Commencement of the French Revolution in 1789 to the Restoration of the Bourbons in 1815. Volume 7. Baudry, Paris.
Alison, A. 1840 History of Europe from the Commencement of the French Revolution in 1789 to the Restoration of the Bourbons in 1815. Volume 8. Blackwood.
Anonymous. 1783 Caricature of the 1783 French Military Mission in Istanbul. Engraving. German.
Anthing, J.F. [Translator] 1813 History of the Campaigns of Count Alexander Suworow Rymnikski. London.
Art Institute of Chicago, 1635. Small Howitzer (Field Cannon) of Artillery Captain Johannes Faulhaber. Reference Number: 1982.3526a-b/.
Askeri Muze [Militarmuseum]. New Order Army Regimental Sultan Selim III Era.
Barbir, K.K. 2014 Ottoman Rule in Damascus, 1708-1758. Princeton University Press.
Basimevi, K. 1997 Tarihten Punumuze Deniz Kuvvetleri Personel Kiyafetlerinin Gecirdigi Asamalar [Ottoman Turkish Navy Organization and Uniforms from 1363 till 1989]. Dz.K.K. Ligi Karargah Basimevi: Ankara.
Borekci, G. 2006 A Contribution to the Military Revolution Debate: The Janissaries' Use of Volley Fire during the Long Ottoman-Habsburg War of 1593-1606 and the Problem of Origins. Acta Orientalia Academiae Scientiarum Hung. Volume 59. Issue 4.
Brenton, E.P. 1837 The Naval History of Great Britain. London: Henry Colburn, Publisher.
Brill, E.J. 1913 [-1936] First Encyclopaedia of Islam.
Browne, W.G. 1799 Travels in Africa, Egypt, and Syria, from the Year 1792 to 1798. London: T. Cadell (Junior), and W. Davies, Strand.
Brindesi, J. Bour, C. (Lithographer) 1850 Choubara Neferi, Soldat of the 1st Reform of Sultan Mahmud II. Illustration. Vinkhuijzen, H.J. [Collection]. New York Public Library [The]. Image ID: 416350.
Brindesi, J. Bour, C. (Lithographer) 1850 Eghri Calpaklissi (Soldat da la Reforme); Choubara Neferi Soldat (1st Reforme). Illustration. Vinkhuijzen, H.J. [Collection]. New York Public Library [The]. Image ID: 416351.
Brindesi, J. Mea, J. 1850 [1855] Elbicei Atika Musee des Anciens Costumes Turcs de Constantinople. Paris: Lemercier.
Brindesi, J. Regnier, C. (Lithographer) 1850 Artilleur-a-Cheval; Yuzbachi, Capitaine d'Infanterie; Artilleur-a-Pied. Lemercier, Paris. Illustration. New York Public Library [The]. Image ID: 85575.
Brindesi, J. Bettannier, J. 1850 (Lithographer) Khoumbardji Bombardiers. Illustration. New York Public Library [The]. Image ID: 85576.
Buyukakca, M.C. 2007 Turkish Army in the Eighteenth Century: War and Military Reform in the Eastern European Context. Graduate Thesis. Middle East Technical University.
Castellan, A-L. 1812 Topdjy Canonnier du Nizam Djedyd; Nefer, Soldat des Nizam Djedyd. Illustrations de Histoire des Othomans. Moeurs, Usages, Costumes des Othomans, et Abrege de Leur Histoire. Paris: Nepveu.
Castellan, A-L. 1797 General Aubert du Bayet Being Received by the Ottoman Grand Vizier in Constantinople in 1796. Painting.
Camden, T. 1814 The History of the Rise, Progress, and Overthrow of Napoleon Bonaparte. J. Stratford.
Cavuszade, H.H. 1721 Ottoman Turks Fighting the Polish Army. Walters Manuscript.
Chambers, E. 1728 Cyclopaedia: or, An Universal Dictionary of Arts and Sciences. Volumes 1/2. London.
Clarke, H. 1816 The History of the War: From the Commencement of the French Revolution to the Present Time. Volume 1. T. Kinnersley.
Coralic, L. 2018 Albanian Soldiers in the Venetian Land Army Across the Adriatic (18th Century). Povijesni Prilozi. Volume 37. Number 54.
Creasy, E.S. 1878 History of the Ottoman Turks: from the Beginning of their Empire to the Present Time. London: R. Bentley.
Dalvimart, O. Miller, W. 1802 The Costume of Turkey: Illustrated by a Series of Engravings; with Descriptions

in English and French. London: T. Bensley.
Dastrup, B.L. 1992 King of Battle: A Branch History of the U.S. Army's Field Artillery. TRADOC Branch History Series.
Dodsley, F. Rivington, C. 1801 The Annual Register, or a View of the History, Politics and Literature of the Year 1799. London.
Douwes, D. 2000 Ottomans in Syria: A History of Justice and Oppression. I.B.Tauris.
Duffy, C. 2005 Military Experience in the Age of Reason. Routledge.
Elgood, R. 1995 Firearms of the Islamic World: In the Tared Rajab Museum, Kuwait. I.B.Tauris.
Eruretin, M. 2001 Osmanli Madalyalari ve Nisanlari [Ottoman Medals and Orders: A Documented History]. DMC.
Eton, W. 1798 A Survey of the Turkish Empire. London: T. Cadell and W. Davies, Strand.
Flaherty, C.J. 1996 Australian Manoeuverist Strategy. Seaview Press.
Fleet, K. Kasaba, R. 2006 The Cambridge History of Turkey. Cambridge University Press.
Garneray, A.L. 1827 [-1830] Battle of Navarino. Painting. Musee de l'Histoire de France (Versailles). Collection Accession Number: MV1795.
Gokcek, M. 2001 Centralization During the Era of Mahmud II. Osmanli Arastirmalari [The Journal of Ottoman Studies] XXI.
Goodwin, G. 2013 The Janissaries. Saqi Books.
Grant, C. 2007 Napoleon's Campaign in Egypt. Volume 2: The British Army and Allies. Partizan Press.
Grehan, J. 2007 Everyday Life and Consumer Culture in Eighteenth-Century Damascus. University of Washington Press.
Gush, G. 1975 Renaissance Armies: 1480 – 1650. PSL, UK.
Henry, C. 2005 English Civil War Artillery 1642-51. Osprey Publishing.
Hochenleitter, L. 1788 Vorstellung der Turkischen Haupt Armee mit 80,000 Mann in Anmarsche bei Sophia in Bulgarien. Illustration.
Howard, E. 1839 Memoirs of Admiral Sir Sidney Smith. Volume 1. R. Bentley.
Hubert, J. 1911 Organization: How Armies are Formed for War. Hard Press Publishing.
Johnson, W.E. Bell, C. 1988 The Ottoman Empire and the Napoleonic Wars. Partizan Press.
Johnson, W.E. 1997 The Sultan's Big Guns: Part I. Online Resource.
Johnson, W.E. 1997 Ottoman Gun Sizes. Online Resource.
Kapidagli, K. 1803 Sultan Selim III in Audience. Painting. Topkapi [Palace Museum].
Kernan, M. 2011 Soldiers of the Ottoman Empire: A Painting Guide by Vexillia Limited (Second Edition). Online Resource.
Kirca, U.D. 2010 The Furious Dogs of Hell: Rebellion, Janissaries and Religion in Sultanic Legitimisation in the Ottoman Empire. Graduate Thesis. Bilgi University.
Knotel, R. 1890 Turkei. Janitscharen. Illustration.
Lapidus, I.M. 2002 A History of Islamic Societies. Cambridge University Press.
Le Prince, J-B. 1770 Polish Janissary. Etching.
Levy, A. [Rothenberg, G.E. et.al. Editors] 1982 Formalization of Cossack Service Under Ottoman Rule. East Central European Society and War. New York: Columbia University Press.
Levy, A. 1982 Military Reform and the Problem of Centralization in the Ottoman Empire in the Eighteenth Century. Middle Eastern Studies. Volume 18.
Losty, J.P. 1989 The Great Gun at Agra. The British Library Journal. Volume 15. Number 1 (Spring).
Low, E.B. MacBride, M. [Edited & Introduction] 1911 With Napoleon at Waterloo. London: Francis Griffiths.
MacFarlane, C. 1829 Constantinople in 1828. London: Saunders and Otley, Conduit Street.
McConnell, D. 1988 British Smooth-Bore Artillery. National Historic Parks and Sites Environment Canada – Parks.
McLean, T. [John Heaviside Clark] 1818 The Military Costume of Turkey. London: Thomas McLean.
Marsigli, L.F. 1732 L'Etat Militaire de l'Empire Ottoman. Amsterdam.
Mazanec, J. 2016 The Ottoman Empire at the Beginning of Tanzimat Reforms. Prague Papers on the History of International Relations 2.
Metropolitan Museum of Art [The]. 1790 French Revolution Cap. Collection Accession Number: 2015.568.
Morier, J.P. 1801 Memoir of a Campaign with the Turkish Army in Egypt, from February to July 1800. London: J. Debrett.
Mostert, N. 2008 Line Upon a Wind: An Intimate History of the Last and Greatest War Fought at Sea Under Sail, 1793-1815. Random House.
Mugnai, B. 2022 The Ottoman Army of the Napoleonic Wars, 1784-1815. Helion & Company.
Mugnai, B. Flaherty, C. 2015 Der Lange Turkenkrieg (1593-1606) Volume 2: The Long Turkish War. Soldiers & Weapons 027. Soldiershop.

Musee de l'Armee [The]. 17th Century (1691) Mortar Mounted on a Cannon Field Carriage with a Single-Block Trail. Inventory Number: 37143.
Musee de l'Armee [The]. 18th Century Ottoman Howitzer.
Nicolle, D. 1995 The Janissaries. Osprey Publishing.
Nicolle, D. 1998 Armies of the Ottoman Empire 1775 - 1820. Osprey Publishing.
Nolan, C.J. 2008 Wars of the Age of Louis XIV, 1650-1715: An Encyclopedia of Global Warfare and Civilization. ABC-CLIO.
Norman, C.A. 1985 Turkish Uniforms of the Crimean Era. Soldiers of the Queen: Issue 85.
Olivier, G.A. 1801 Travels in the Ottoman Empire, Egypt, and Persia, Undertaken by Order of the Government of France, During the First Six Years of the Republic. Volumes 1-2. London: T.N. Longman, O. Rees, Paternoster-Row, T. Cadell (Junior), W. Davies.
Orenc, A.F. 2012 Albanian Soldiers in the Ottoman Army During the Greek Revolt at 1821. 2nd International Balkan Annual Conference.
Phillips, R. [Editor] 1803 The Monthly Magazine, or, British Register, Volume 16. Part 2. London: J. Adland.
Poqueville, F.C.H.L. 1806 Travels Through the Morea, Albania, and Other Parts of the Ottoman Empire to Constantinople, During the Years 1798, 1799, 1800, and 1801. London: R. Phillips
Quataert, D. 1997 Clothing Laws, State, and Society in the Ottoman Empire, 1720-1829. International Journal of Middle East Studies, Volume 29. Number 3 (August).
Radcliffe, J.N. 1858 The Hygiene of the Turkish Army: Report with Additions, from The Sanitary Review. John Churchill. New Burlington Street: London.
Raif, M. [Efendi] 1798 Tableau des Nouveaux Reglemens de L'Empire Ottoman. Constantinople.
Reid, J.J. 2000 Crisis of the Ottoman Empire: Prelude to Collapse 1839-1878. Franz Steiner Verlag.
Ralamb, C. 1658 [-1657]. Deli Cavalryman, with Tiger Skin and Holding a Decapitated Captive Head. Ralamb Costume Book. Royal Library in Stockholm.
Rogge, C. 2013 Prussian 18th Century Artillery. Smoothbore Ordnance Journal.
Roubicek, M. 1978 Modern Turkish Troops, 1797-1915: In Contemporary Pictures. Franciscan Printing Press.
Roy, K. 2011 War, Culture and Society in Early Modern South Asia, 1740-1849. Routledge.
Sadat, D.R. 1972 Rumeli Ayanlari: The Eighteenth Century. The Journal of Modern History. Volume 44. Number 3 (September).
Sakul, K. [Fynn-Paul, J. Editor] 2014 The Evolution of Ottoman Military Logistics System in the Later Eighteenth Century: The Rise of a New Class of Military Entrepreneur. War, Entrepreneurs, and the State in Europe and the Mediterranean, 1300-1800. Brill.
Sakul, K. [Lenman, B.P. Editor] 2013 Military Engineering in the Ottoman Empire. Military Engineers and the Development of the Early-Modern European State. Dundee University Press.
Sakul, K. 2012 What Happened to Pouqueville's Frenchmen? Ottoman Treatment of the French Prisoners During the War of the Second Coalition (1798-1802). Turkish Historical Review 3.
Sakul, K. 2012 Ottoman Perceptions of the Military Reforms of Tipu Sultan and Sahin Giray. 20th CIEPO Symposium: Rethymno (27 June – 1 July).
Sakul, K. [Gonergun, F. Raina, D. Editors] 2011 General Observations on the Ottoman Military Industry, 1774- 1839. Problems of Organization and Standardization Europe and Asia: Historical Studies on the Transmission, Adoption and Adaptation of Knowledge. Springer.
Scott, W. 1827 The Life of Napoleon Bonaparte. Volume VI. Paris: A. and W. Galignani.
Sevket, M. [Mahmud Chevket Pasha] 1907 L'Organization et les Uniformes de l'Armee Ottomanne. Premiere Partie.
Shaw, S.J. Shaw, E.K. 1977 History of the Ottoman Empire and Modern Turkey; Reform, Revolution, and Republic: The Rise of Modern Turkey 1808-1975. Volume 2. Cambridge University Press.
Shaw, S.J. 1969 Selim III and the Ottoman Navy. Klincksieck.
Shaw, S.J. 1965 The Nizam-i Cedid Army Under Sultan Selim III 1789-1807. Oriens. Volumes 18/19 (1965/1966).
Shaw, S.J. 1965 The Origins of Ottoman Military Reform: The Nizam-i Cedid Army of Sultan Selim III. The Journal of Modern History. Volume 37. Number 3 (September).
Slade, A. 1867 Turkey and the Crimean War: A Narrative of Historical Events. London: Smith, Elder & Company.
Stolpe, E. 1985 Klassizismus un Krieg, Uberden Historien-Mater Jacques–Louis David. Frankfurt and New York: Campus Verlag.
Suleyman. 1526 Sultan Suleiman During the Battle of Mohacs. Topkapi Palace Museum, Istanbul.
Sunar, M.M. 2006 Cauldron of Dissent: A Study of the Janissary Corps, 1807-1826. Binghamton University Dissertation.

Szatmary, C. [Popp de] 1848 Non-Commissioned Officer of the Day Reports [Field Cannon in Background]. Album: The Drawings of Uniforms and Arms of the Turkish Troops. State Hermitage Museum. Collection Number: ЭРВГ-3433.

Szatmary, C. [Popp de] 1848 [Turkish] Cannon. Album: The Drawings of Uniforms and Arms of the Turkish Troops. State Hermitage Museum. Collection Number: ЭРВГ-3448.

Tooke, W. 1801 View of the Russian Empire, During the Reign of Catharine the Second, and to the Close of the Eighteenth Century. Volume 2. Dublin: P. Wogan.

Topkapi [Palace Museum]. Hazine. 1609 Mezokeresztes, 1596. Turkish Miniature, 16th Century. Istanbul.

Tott [de], F. Peyssonnel [de], M. 1786 Memoirs of Baron De Tott; Strictures and Remarks on the Memoirs of Baron De Tott. London: G.G.J. and J. Robinson.

Tyrrell, F. H. 1910 Old Turkish Military Costumes and Standards. The Imperial and Asiatic, Quarterly Review and Oriental and Colonial Record. Third Series. Volume 30. Numbers 59/60 (July-October).

Unknown. 1788 Turkisch Kaiserliche Artillerie. Illustration. Vinkhuijzen, H.J. [Collection]. New York Public Library [The]. Image ID: 416254.

Unknown. 1805 [1600-1805] Leventi. Illustration. Vinkhuijzen, H.J. [Collection]. New York Public Library [The]. Image ID: 416281.

Unknown. 1810 [-1817] Mahmud II Grand Review. Illustration. Vinkhuijzen, H.J. [Collection]. New York Public Library [The]. Image ID: 416284.

Unknown. 1810 [-1817] Mahmud II Grand Review. Illustration. Vinkhuijzen, H.J. [Collection]. New York Public Library [The]. Image ID: 416289.

Unknown. 1815 [-1820] Turkish Canonnier. Illustration. Vinkhuijzen, H.J. [Collection]. New York Public Library [The]. Image ID: 418607.

Unknown. 1828 Turkey. Soldier of the Galeongees, or Marine Corps. Illustration. Vinkhuijzen, H.J. [Collection]. New York Public Library [The]. Image ID: 435679.

Unknown. 1830 [-1849] Troupes Regulieres Turques – Artillerie: Artilleur-a-Cheval. Illustration. Vinkhuijzen, H.J. [Collection]. New York Public Library [The]. Image ID: 418830.

Unknown. 1830 [-1849] Soldier of the Bostandjees, or Corps from the Sultan's Gardeners. Illustration. Vinkhuijzen, H.J. [Collection]. New York Public Library [The]. Image ID: 418825.

Unknown. 1830 [-1849] Bimbachi: Chef de Bataillon du la Ref du Sultan Selim. Illustration. Vinkhuijzen, H.J. [Collection]. New York Public Library [The]. Image ID: 418804.

Unknown. 1832 Officiers des Canonniers. Illustration. Vinkhuijzen, H.J. [Collection]. New York Public Library [The]. Image ID: 418805.

Uyar, M. Erickson. E.J. 2009 A Military History of the Ottomans: From Osman to Ataturk. ABCCLIO.

Valentini, G.W. [Anonymous Translator] 1828 Military Reflections on Turkey. C. & J. Rivington: London.

Vanmour, J-B, Scotin, G. (Engraver) 1714 Saka, Charitable Derviche Qui Porte de l'Eau Par la Ville et la Donne par Charite [Saka, Charitable Dervish Who Carries Water Through the City and Gives it Out of Charity]. L. Cars, Paris. Illustration. New York Public Library [The]. Image ID: 94402.

Vivien, H. 1900 Costumes Militaires. Paris.

Walsh, T. 1803 Journal of the Late Campaign in Egypt. Cadell & Davies, Strand, London.

War Office [The]. 2008 [The] 1915 Notes on the Turkish Army: With a Short Vocabulary of Turkish Words and Phrases. N & M Press.

Watts, R.D. 1997 The Turkish Army of the 18th Century. Agema Publications.

Wittman, W. 1803 Travels in Turkey, Asia-Minor, Syria, and Across the Desert into Egypt During the Years 1799, 1800, and 1801, in Company with the Turkish Army, and the British Military Mission. London: Richard Phillips.

Wright, J. 1799 History of the Life and Campaigns of Count Alexander Suworow Rymnikski. Publisher: J. Wright, London.

Yesil, F. 2016 Ihtilaller Caginda Osmanli Ordusu [The Ottoman Army in the Age of Revolutions: A Study on Socio-economic and Sociopolitical Change in the Ottoman Empire (1793-1826)]. History Foundation Yurt Publishing.

Yesil, F. 2009 The Transformation of the Turkish Army from Nizam-i Cedid to the Abolition of the Janissaries (1789-1826). Ph.D. Thesis. University of Hacettepe.

Yildiz, A. 2017 Crisis and Rebellion in the Ottoman Empire: The Downfall of a Sultan in the Age of Revolution. Bloomsbury Publishing.

Yildiz, A. 2012 The Anatomy of a Rebellious Social Group: The Yamaks of the Bosporus at the Margins of Ottoman Society. Crete University Press.

Zurcher, E.J. 1999 Arming the State: Military Conscription in the Middle East and Central Asia, 1775-1925. I.B.Tauris.

CONTENTS

Timeline 3

Introduction 5

Chapter 1: New Order Army Uniforms 8

Chapter 2: Officers' Ranks and Insignia 17

Chapter 3: Generalship and Officers' Command 19

Chapter 4: Standing Army's Tactics 26

Chapter 5: Infantry Organization 38

Chapter 6: Infantry Soldier's Weapons and Equipment 48

Chapter 7: Topchees: Artillery and New Order Army Regimental Cannon Buluks: Company 52

Chapter 8: Humbaraci: Bombardiers 63

Chapter 9: Arnaut Infantry 67

Chapter 10: Galeonjees: New Order Army Marine Regiments 70

Chapter 11: Saka and Imam 71

Chapter 12: 1806 Edirne Rebellion 73

Chapter 13: The 1807 End 77

References 82

OTHER TITLES BY THE SAME AUTHOR

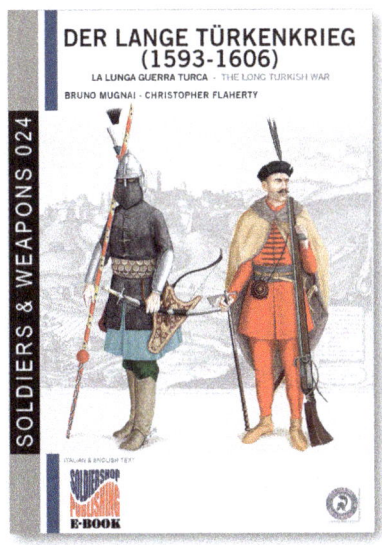

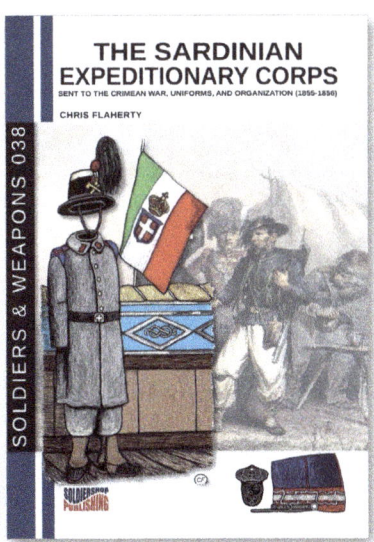
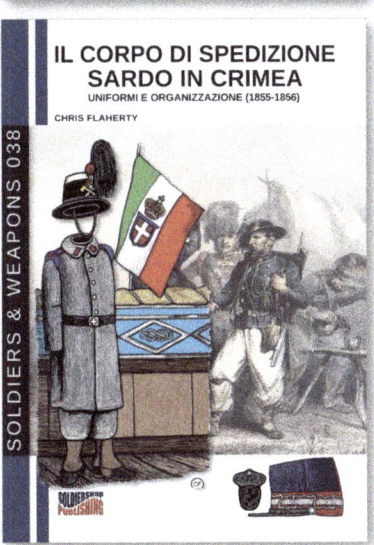
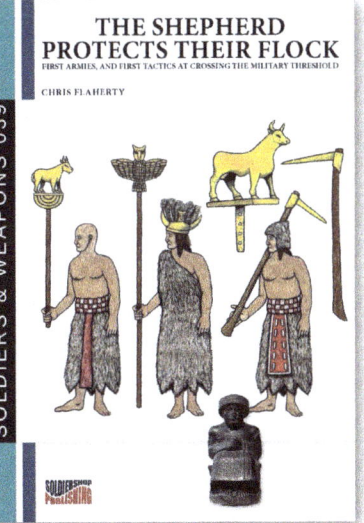
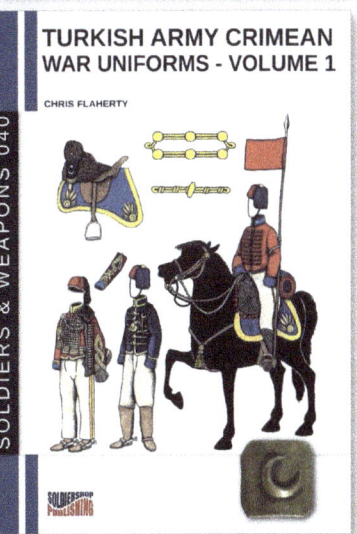
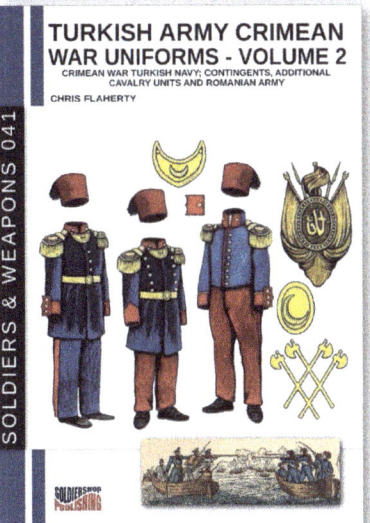
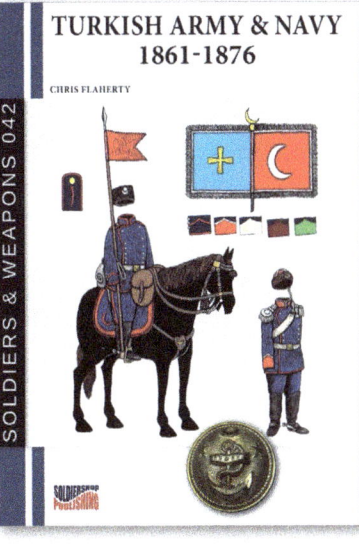
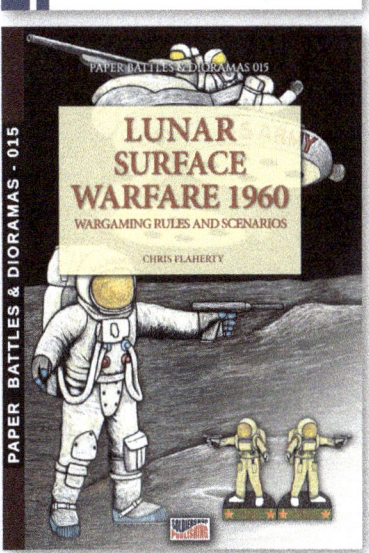

SOLDIERS&WEAPONS 049

www.ingramcontent.com/pod-product-compliance
Lightning Source LLC
LaVergne TN
LVHW072124060526
838201LV00069B/4968